C000319047

Walking In My Sleep

A Hampshire childhood in Peace and War: 1938 to 1942

by

Jane Chichester

Red'n'Ritten Ltd.

Published by Red'n'Ritten Ltd, 17 Kings Barn Lane,
Steyning, West Sussex BN44 3YR
© Red'n'Ritten Ltd. 2003

All rights reserved. No part of this publication may be reproduced in any material form whether by photocopying or storing in any medium by electronic means (whether or not transiently or incidentally to some other use of this publication) without the prior written consent of the copyright owner except in accordance with the provisions of the Copyright, designs and Patents Act 1988. Applications for the copyright owner's written permission to reproduce any part of this publication should be addressed to the Publisher.

WARNING: The doing of any unauthorised act in relation to this work may result in both civil and criminal liability.

No responsibility for the loss occasioned to any person acting or refraining from acting as a result of the material contained in this publication will be accepted by the authors or publishers.

ISBN 1 904278 30 2
A CIP Catalogue record for this book is available from the British Library.

Printed by Apollo Press, Worthing, West Sussex.
Cover Artwork and Illustrations by Mike Avery.

FOREWORD

The Second World War disrupted many people's lives in terrible ways. This memoir tells the story of how it affected a child of nine, although the only shots she heard fired were those of her father shooting pheasants.

Jane is enjoying an idyllic country childhood when the story begins. Untroubled by any formal education or adult supervision she fills her days with her animals, imaginary companions and the eccentric people who live or work on the farm. She observes her glamorous parent's parties with a critical eye, but they are not part of her life. At night she sleep walks.

When war breaks out this peaceful existence is shattered by the arrival of a family of female cousins who move in for the duration. They bring with them a governess, and therefore discipline, timetables and regular meals. This enchanting book, sometimes sad, and sometimes hilarious, tells how she comes to terms with an invasion, which she sees as bad as any going on across the Channel.

It is the story of a vanished world, which many older readers may recognise, and in which many younger ones would wish to live.

Biography:

Jane Chichester was herself brought up in the country and wrote her first book at the age of nine. She is the published author of four novels and several short stories. Now a widow, she was married to the writer Roger Longrigg for forty-three years and still lives in her beloved Hampshire, not far from her childhood home.

Jane visits Mr. Delitz in the barn

PART ONE

Chapter One

The fishing hut was octagonal in shape and built of wood. Inside it was a cool refuge from the hot summer's day outside and had a pungent smell of river mud, wet dogs and thick green juicy reeds. Watery reflections bounced off the clear surface of the chalk stream flowing past, and danced on the walls.

At noon it was full of the sound of the heavy boots of our father and his friends and their talk and laughter as they stacked their rods and dumped the creels with the resigned-looking dead trout in them. Howell and Juffs, the water keepers, would have their sandwiches down there with the dead fish and the rods and landing nets, while the fishermen tramped up the wide wooden ladder to the upper room where our mother and Karin had set out the picnic lunch on the big round table.

There was cold chicken, and ham crusted with brown sugar and cloves, a blue veined Stilton, baskets of bread and fruit, and flagons of beer and cider. Above the windows, which flashed with the sunlight off the river, the bare wooden ceiling sloped upwards like the inside of a tent.

I took my lunch out on to the balcony and sat with my legs dangling over the glass-clear water of the stew-pond below. The wood of the balcony felt warm and scratchy to my bare legs.

Aged eight, I was to all intents and purposes a boy and wore a blue aertex shirt, grey flannel shorts and a blue and red belt with a snake buckle. In my pockets I had a catapult, a penknife, a hoof-pick and some pieces of string. Sitting down was quite uncomfortable, like squatting on a scrap heap.

Behind me the sound of the grown-ups' lunch was getting louder, cutlery clattered on plates, glasses clinked and voices quacked like ducks on a pond. My sister, Imogen, came out on to the balcony carrying a large plate piled high with bread and cheese. Three years older than me, she was very tall for her age and was supposed to have out-grown her strength. We quarrelled a lot, and when she tried to push me into the slurry butt at home, she seemed to have plenty of strength left. Her long hair was tied back in two plaits and today she was wearing a cotton dress that was too small for her.

"They're getting awfully noisy in there," she said.

"So I can hear, it's probably the cider."

I looked down through the bars of the balcony at the shadowy shapes of big stockfish lying far below in their secret watery world. I tossed a pellet of bread down to them and immediately the mirror cracked as a flurry of silver heads broke the surface. Then with a flick of their tails they were gone again, leaving lazy concentric circles behind them widening out towards the banks.

Dinah, our black Labrador puppy, came and sat beside me, showing a toothy smile and thumping the wooden floor of the balcony with her tail.

"I suppose you think you're a fish," I said, giving her a bit of bread.

In the afternoon when everyone was dispersing to their various beats, Karin said she wanted to fish to find out if it was as boring as it looked. She was tall with long blonde hair and had a stronger character than our mother, who was left behind in the hut to clear up the lunch. Our mother was also tall and blonde, but in a different way.

"Come with me, my dear. I will show you that it is not at all boring," Uncle Joe volunteered.

Karin was supposed to be our governess. She had answered an advertisement in 'The Lady' for someone to come and look after us as our parents were often away, either staying with friends in sporty house-parties or abroad on business. Karin had sent a full-length photograph with her reply, showing her standing wearing a slinky black suit with one knee slightly bent and a saucy little hat tipped over one eye.

"We'll have her." My father didn't hesitate for a moment. She had been with us for about six months.

I followed Karin and Uncle Joe along the riverbank, with Dinah, treading carefully so as not to disturb the fish. I saw the bright arrow of a kingfisher skim the surface of the water. Hatches of fly hung in the still air like dancing nets.

Uncle Joe put his arm round the beautiful Swede to show her how to keep her wrist straight when she cast. Her line fell with a splash in midstream and a startled moorhen hurried away.

"Ach, it is so stupid with the little fly," she complained in her Greta Garbo voice. "With some brown bread it would be easy."

"Dry fly fishing is an art, my dear. Try again."

Soon the fly got caught up in the branches of a willow tree, whose gnarled and tortured trunk hung over the river like one of the Arthur Rackham drawings in my fairy story books. From where I crouched in the fragrant grass of the water meadow I watched them trying to disentangle it; they seemed to giggle a lot. Beside me Dinah began to pant, her long pink tongue hanging dripping out of her mouth, and the sun was hot on the back of my neck.

I heard Uncle Joe say. "Just a taste. There'd be no harm in it, no-one would find out."

I wondered if they were going to have another picnic, so soon after lunch.

On the next beat a different kind of fishing was going on. I went and joined our father who was standing casting a line, as fine as a thread of gossamer; the fly landed on the water as delicately as a real fly.

Just over six feet tall with wings of black hair touched with grey at the temples, he could have been a heron standing there at the edge of the reeds. A little to his left, Howell, the water keeper, who resembled a red-faced suet pudding in his tweed hat and knickerbocker suit, waited steady as a rock, with the landing net. The only sound was the gentle ticking of our father's reel and the whistle of the line as he whipped it back and forth.

Once more he laid the fly gently on the water, and this time there was a small gulp, and suddenly the line was singing out of the reel and there was a trout, thrashing, pulling and diving about in the river, fighting for its life. I held my breath as our father raised the point of his rod and began to reel in; soon the fish was being towed inexorably towards the bank and the now kneeling Howell ready with the landing net. One scoop into the water and there it lay, mouth gasping, mother-of-pearl sides heaving, at the bottom of the net. A tap on the head with the 'priest' and it was still.

Howell bent over the fish, carefully removing the fly from its mouth. Our father turned and saw me for the first time, his blue eyes shining. "Hello, darling! That was exciting wasn't it? Now let's see if we can get another. Try the same fly again shall we, Howell?"

"Reckon so, sir. If that's what they're taking, that's what they're taking."

By the time two more fish lay on the bank, our father was bored. Although a keen sportsman, he had a restless nature and needed frequent changes of scene, company and occupation. Our mother, who was happy to spend whole days by herself, quietly gardening, found his life-style rather exhausting.

"That's enough of that. Time for tea," and carrying his rod, he strode off along the path back to the fishing hut. There would be time enough for a set or two of tennis before dinner.

Howell and I struggled to keep up. The keeper was a good friend of mine and in the spring had made me the catapult, which now hung out of the back pocket of my shorts.

"You hit anything with that catapult yet, Miss Jane?" he asked as we skirted the willows where Karin had got so hung up. There was no sign of her and Uncle Joe now.

"Yes, I hit one of the bantams, but it was by mistake. I was really aiming at a blackbird in the fruit cage."

"You just keep your eye on the target."

"I do try. I think I'm getting better." I felt the catapult in my back pocket and adopted the swagger of a cowboy with a six-gun at his side.

Back at the turbine hut shouts of laughter broke the evening stillness. Karin had gone off on her own and caught one of the big, fat, lazy stockfish with some brown bread and a bent pin, as she had threatened to do. Uncle Joe was chuckling as he weighed it on his 'Pocket Samson'. "Five pounds! What a whopper!"

Our father looked severely at the cock fish as it hung on the scale, its bottom jaw open showing its teeth. It certainly was very large. The laughter checked. "You're a very naughty girl, Karin. Better not let the keepers see or there'll be hell to pay."

"I'm so sorry, I didn't know," though she did not look particularly sorry.

Going home in the crowded car, I sat in front on Uncle Joe's lap, enveloped in the smell of hot tweed. He began to sing quietly, rocking backwards and forwards.

"I love a lassie,
A bonny Swedish lassie,
She's as sweet as the heather in the dell..."

"Shut up, Joe, you old rogue," said our father as he negotiated the narrow track that led away from the river. I looked out of the window, back to where the swallows were swooping low over the water in and out of the shadows of the willow trees, practising acrobatic turns in the evening light.

Most of the men who came to stay for those summer weekends seemed to fall in love with Karin and she had little time left over from flirting with them to be our governess, which suited me. Sometimes in the mornings she tried to teach us German, if she could find us, and in the evenings she was supposed to see that I at least went to bed on time.

One Saturday evening I was on the fore-deck of my ship, H.M.S. Dalasenus, which to adult eyes was a sycamore tree growing by the dell at the far end of the garden. Below me to the right the grown-ups were playing tennis; to me the sound of tennis balls hitting gut was the noise of muffled gunfire. To the left, smooth green waves of lawn and froth of shrubs lapped the sides of our old white farmhouse as it lay basking in the light of the setting sun.

"Fire!" I shouted, and a depth charge flew through the wall that bordered the iris garden and buried itself in the thatch of the Elizabethan tithe barn beyond.

"A direct hit, sir," said my number one.

"Good show."

Puffing at my pipe, I glanced down through the dense green leaves and caught sight of Karin's rather large Swedish feet far below.

"Jane, darling, come down now. I know that you are up there; it is your bedtime."

Pock, pock, pock went the tennis balls.

"Swedish destroyer on the starboard bow!" sang out the lookout from the crow's nest.

"Starboard a point, Mr. Mate," I snapped.

"Starboard a point it is, sir."

"Have you got their range?"

"Aye, aye sir."

"Ready, aim, fire!"

"Jane, darling, I will count to three, if you are not down by then you will go without your supper."

"Good shooting, Mr. Mate, those turnips won't trouble us again. I think I'll turn in now. Rouse me if anything unforeseen should occur."

"Aye, aye sir."

I saluted my shipmates and went below, knowing that I was leaving my vessel in good hands.

"Three," said Karin as I landed beside her.

"We were in the middle of a battle," I grumbled, hopping along two steps to her one on the way back to the house.

"Who was winning?"

"We were, of course."

"Good."

Later, as I lay in bed with the curtains drawn – thin blue cotton ones that hardly dimmed the golden trumpet call of the evening sky – our parents and some of the grown-ups came in to say goodnight on their way down to dinner. The women looked very glamorous and smelt delicious as they bent and kissed me.

Our father stood by the window smoking a cigarette. I began to bounce about on my bed. "A story! A story! Mummy, tell me a story!"

"Now don't get over-excited. Be a good girl and get to sleep. I'll tell you a story tomorrow."

They were leaving. Like swallows, the grown-ups swooped in and out of our lives.

"Don't go! What's that shiny thing in your hair, Mummy?"

"A diamond as big as the Ritz." My father picked me up and swung me round and put me back to bed. "Goodnight, darling. Goodnight."

At the door someone asked, *sotto voce*: "Does she still - wander?"

"I'm afraid so," answered our mother.

"She'll grow out of it."

"I hope you're right."

They were gone, swishing their slippery dresses down the stairs, leaving the smell of their scent hanging on the air. A thread of our father's cigarette smoke clung to the curtain as though from a genie's lamp.

My sister Imogen, who slept in the room across the passage, put her head round the door. "I'll tell you when the main course comes out."

"Right."

I lay listening to the sounds of the house. The last of the bath water gurgling down through the drainpipes. Mrs. Dowling, the cook, banging the doors of the Aga and squabbling with Hansi and Bertha, the two Austrian maids. Somebody sounding the gong and the muffled rumble of the grown-ups moving into the dining room. Popping of corks and sleep-making resonance of adult conversation.

The golden evening turned my ceiling to dusty apricot. A bantam cock gave a last squeaky crow as it settled down to roost in the Macrocarpa by the stables. I dozed off.

"Psst! It's coming out!"

Eyes heavy with sleep, I sat with Imogen at the top of the back stairs. We were just out of sight of Mrs. Dowling and the maids, but with a clear view of the magic casement – the sliding hatch into the dining room. Through it, unseen hands passed half-empty dishes of roast duckling, petit-pois and tiny carrots tossed in butter. Timing our run to perfection, we sped down the green linoleumed stairs and carried off the most succulent morsels.

Back again in my room and joined by Imogen's dog Brora, we sat on my bed.

"Yummy. What's for pudding do you think?" I asked as we licked our fingers.

"Stay here. I'll go and see." My sister came back with a little dish of peaches in brandy and cream. I already had hiccups.

"Hansi caught me, but she gave me some all the same."

"Hic! It tastes rather funny."

"That's the brandy, stupid. I suppose you're really too young to be drinking alcohol."

Smoke from the battlefield billowed round me. It felt like a huge black cloud. I was trapped in it, suffocating, and the more I tried to extricate myself the more it pressed in on me from all sides. Whichever way I turned, the darkness enveloped me. I fought back, desperately, trying to scream for help, but no sound came. I gasped for breath, knowing that I was going to die.

Karin's soothing voice came through the blackness and the light went on. I stood there, in the airing cupboard, smothered by all the linen and towels I had pulled off the shelves. "My darling, what are you doing in here? Come to Karin, why, you're shivering!" and she put her arms round me and held me tight. "It's all right, Karin is here. Let's go back to bed."

Karin sat on my bed and sang a Swedish lullaby, still holding me. Her voice was deep and comforting. Long after I stopped shaking I made her stay with me, so as not to be alone in the dark.

The house party left on Monday morning. Some of the departing guests not only tipped Mrs. Dowling and the maids, but also Imogen and me. One of our favourites was a bachelor called D'Arcy Collis who always gave us a five-pound note as big as a white table napkin. He looked like the actor George Saunders, and liked to tease our father on the state of the place.

"Ah," he would say, turning in at the gate on arrival. "The drive, approach or puddled way," and check his tyres ostentatiously for punctures. He also teased our mother. "Poor Myra, no personality of her own. She's just a pale shadow of her husband," which was only partly true.

Some of the more annoying guests ruffled our hair. I kept clear of the one who had left his glass eye on the bathroom windowsill overnight, in case he took it out again. On Friday night his wife had made herself unpopular by winning four pounds off our mother at backgammon, and then retiring to bed for the rest of the weekend, apparently too ill for a return game. And there was a beautiful redhead called Ruth Glover, who could improvise on the piano by the hour.

When they had all gone our mother dusted off her hands in a conclusive gesture and went back indoors. I decided to go and see the Professor who lived in the barn. I pulled open the wrought iron gate with its intricate bunches of iron grapes and vine leaves that led to the upper garden where the barn and stables were. The rusty hinges gave a kind of creaking groan. On either side the long wall was smothered in honeysuckle and rambler roses, and alive with the hum of bees busy in the flowers.

Mr. Delitz

Leo Delitz was an Austrian artist and former Professor who had come to stay for the weekend two years ago, and had been spending the summer with us ever since. He had painted a flattering portrait of our handsome father, and spent many hours sketching us and the ponies, and pastoral scenes around the place. It was a relief to our mother when he decided to make a home for himself in the barn, as the amount of painting paraphernalia that he brought with him was gradually taking over the house.

To me the camp he made there was an endless source of fascination: there was an iron bedstead, an easel, a tin bath behind a wobbly screen, stacks of canvases, clotted palettes, jam-jars full of paint brushes and a Primus stove with battered, blackened cooking utensils. He lived the kind of life I would have lived, if I had not been so hung about with civilisation.

Now, I found him cooking his breakfast, a very grey porridge, which must have been heavily flavoured with paraffin fumes. Unlike anyone else I know he ate it with black currant jam; we had treacle on ours.

"So, here is little Jane come to visit old Delitz." He glanced at me over the rim of his wire-framed spectacles as he stirred the mixture with a wooden spoon. His head was bald on top, but quite a lot of hair stuck out at the sides and round the back. "Would you like some porridge?"

"No, thank you. I've had it. Daddy says in Scotland men eat their porridge standing up, in case their enemies attack them while they are sitting down."

"The Scots are a savage race," he said in his high-pitched old man's voice. "In Austria we do not have this problem. If our enemies wish to attack us we challenge them to a duel, between meals."

He sat down in the battered armchair and began to eat the mauve mixture. I went across to the far wall to inspect the baby owls.

This part of the barn had a false ceiling made, long ago, from huge sheets of canvas, now stiff with the droppings of the numerous owls that lived above, under the rafters. Most days, several of their offspring fell through the holes in the canvas, and these Mr. Delitz would revive with porridge and black currant jam, and sometimes even drops of brandy, before bedding them down in straw-lined cardboard boxes. At night their parents breathed heavily in the roof like snoring ghosts; some of them also nested in chimneys in the house, giving visitors a nasty shock if they were not forewarned.

"There are four more since yesterday," I said, watching the babies as they sat in their boxes with their eyes closed, trembling a little in their white fur coats.

"Yes. The parents are very careless. I see you have brought your catapult, little Jane. We will go and paint the cows and when they fall asleep you can hit them, ping! with a stone to restore the lifelike expression." The smell of coffee rose above the paraffin fumes and he filled his cup.

"Well. I haven't hit very much, so far."

"A cow is a large target." He began to get his painting things together, and threw the coffee grounds onto the floor. "You can carry the umbrella and the stool."

"I don't think it's going to rain." He had a large multi-coloured umbrella, which I knew from experience was extremely heavy.

"It is also for the shade."

In the long meadow beyond the house and the garden the cows were lying about chewing their mid-morning cud. Mr. Delitz set up his easel in the middle of them, opened out his camp stool and stuck the umbrella into its tripod. He polished his spectacles on a filthy handkerchief and then set about choosing paints from the big wooden box filled with little tubes; as he squeezed them onto the palette, constantly checking his models as he did so, his cheeks, with their several days' growth of grizzled beard, quivered with creative fervour.

The cows loved being painted. They arranged themselves in languorous attitudes round his stool, jaws chomping, eyelashes fluttering.

"That one there, my dear," he said, after a while. "The one that looks like Claudette Colbert; you see the one I mean?" He pointed with his brush. "She is getting drowsy. Hit her with your catapult, that will wake her up."

I loaded the sling with a small stone and took careful aim. A hit! My first. The cow glanced round haughtily as the pebble bounced off her flank and then resumed staring at Mr. Delitz, masticating rhythmically.

"Good shot."

"Thank you."

On the canvas the pastoral scene began to take shape. Mr. Delitz hummed contentedly as he blocked in the billowing trees in the distance that seemed about to sail away over the gentle waves of grass. His curvaceous style had been known to offend his human models. Karin had torn up a portrait he had done of her, which made her look like an old Austrian haus-frau with a double chin.

"Would you like me to wake up anybody else?" Legs apart, I flexed the sling of my catapult. I felt that I could hit anything – a Red Indian, a snipe, a tiger.

"No, mein liebchen, for a moment I do not need your services."

I slipped away.

From a distance the artist, sitting under his gaily-striped umbrella surrounded by his more or less attentive models, looked like some eccentric professor bringing learning to the ruminant classes.

Between the back door and the coal shed our Muscovy ducks, Shadrack, Meshag and Abednego, shuffled furtively along, rolling their eggs towards some secret hiding place with their long beaks.

"Hocca, hocca, hocca!" they protested, as I shooed them away and picked up the still-warm eggs.

"I'm sorry, but Mrs. Dowling needs these eggs, you know."

"Hocca, hocca, hocca!"

They shook their red wattles at me and shuffled off in a new direction. I put the eggs in the wooden bowl on the shelf just inside the back door. A snatch of Strauss came from an open window over my head as Hansi, the maid, fluttered a feather duster in the air, describing graceful circles.

I wondered whether she was signalling to Harold, the farmer's son, with whom Imogen and I were sure she was planning to elope. She was very pretty with pink cheeks and curly, honey-coloured hair; both she and Bertha wore blue and white striped dresses to do the housework in the mornings, but Hansi's was much tighter across the bodice.

Once, on returning from a ride, I had found her with Harold behind the barn; they had inspired Imogen to invent some splendid stories of secret love in the manner of whichever book she was reading at the time – say, Tess of the D'Urbervilles or Lorna Doone – and tell to me when we were riding or on the nights when I could not sleep.

"Hello, Hansi! Is Karin looking for me?" I called up to her. Sometimes I had lessons in the mornings.

"Nein, Miss Jane, Miss Sandberg is lying down." She passed a plump pink hand over her forehead. "She has a terrible headache – no lesson today!" Her laughter tinkled down the sunny white side of the house like bells.

In the orchard I found Vince, the odd job man, scything the grass between the fruit trees. Every dozen strokes or so he would stop and sharpen the scythe with the stone that he kept in his pocket. The blade shone like silver and was as sharp as a razor, or so he said. Against one of the trees lay the knapsack containing his lunch and a flagon of cider, which I knew from experience he could down at one draught, without swallowing. We had a special relationship.

"Good morning, Sir Charles," I said, when he paused to sharpen the scythe.

"Well now, and good morning to you, your ladyship." He took off his cap and mopped his forehead, white as a mushroom underneath. He had a lean, handsome face with a droopy moustache stained brown in the middle by tobacco. "And what have you been-a-doing of, this fine morning?"

"Oh, this and that. Shooting a few cows, that sort of thing."

"Did you hit one with that ole catapult, then?"

"Yes. Mr. Delitz asked me to."

"Well." He replaced the cap after giving his head a scratch. "Them old cows. Reckon that gave 'er a start."

"It did rather. Have you found any more wasps nests?" I looked about, sniffing the honeyed smell of the newly cut grass.

"Arh. There's one under that ole greengage. We'll deal with 'im directly, when I've finished this yere grass." He spat on his hands and began scything again, swinging the blade in an arc round his legs, laying the grass down in silky rows; the mermaid tattoo on his right forearm swung, too, as though she were swimming under water.

I found the entrance to the wasp nest under the greengage tree, a small round hole up and down which the wasps danced, carrying their secrets.

"We're going to get you," I told them. "Reckon you'll all be dead, directly."

In the kitchen garden Mr. Kilmaster, the gardener, was tying the tomato plants to their poles and snipping off the tender shoots in their armpits. He wore a green baize apron with a kangaroo pocket full of raffia, and a pork-pie hat on the back of his head; his round fat face was red and sweaty.

I did not have the special relationship with him that I had with Vince, and today I waited in the shadow of the long line of loose boxes, which stretched between the kitchen garden and the tithe barn, where Mr. Delitz lived, until I saw him set off for the house with the big trug full of vegetables that he had picked earlier. Every morning he carried the day's crop down to the back door in time to join Mrs. Dowling and his wife, Mrs. Kilmaster, for their interminable 'elevenses' round the kitchen table. Mrs. Kilmaster was built like a small barn and had her hair permed into a sort of corrugated iron roof; later she would prepare the vegetables and scour Mrs. Dowling's pots and pans.

When he had gone, I helped myself to some carrots and cabbage leaves for my guinea pigs, Hazel and Doris. I lay down beside their cage, on a patch of grass in front of the stables, and watched them eating, their teeth working like tiny chain saws while they held the carrots in their pink paws.

It was peaceful now that the weekend visitors had gone. Outside the saddle-room door, where Imogen was getting her chestnut mare, Thea, ready for a ride, the Chinese bantams were busy scratching about for hay seeds in the dust – two steps forward, peck, peck, two steps back – their feathered legs making them look like clumsy rumba dancers. One of the barn cats slunk by in the shade of the Macrocarpa, eyeing them, and the cocks screeched in mock alarm, interrupting the dance.

Imogen rode past; Thea's hoof beats momentarily disturbing the bantams again. "I've caught Robin, he's in the stable. The flies are awful in the field."

"Thanks. I might catch you up later." I said.

The summer day stretched ahead, blissfully free of any adult interference.

Chapter Two

Although our parents only rented our farmhouse and no land went with it, except for the nine acres of garden and orchard, Imogen and I considered the large estate, which surrounded it to be our own property. We had names for every coppice, wood and field through which we rode our ponies during most of the daylight hours.

Some of it was Red Indian Country, which would have surprised the farmer and his family who lived peacefully at the bottom of Dead Man's Gulch. Flights of arrows had to be dodged as we galloped home from Medicine Hat through Kicking Horse Pass. A gibbet swung from a lonely cross-roads and in Highwayman's wood ghosts shook the trees in Autumn, sending the dry leaves clattering down to the ground where they turned into tumbleweed tornadoes whirling past the ponies' legs.

Sometimes our rides took us to one of the three villages, which formed the points of the triangle of which our house was the centre, separated from each by five miles of open country.

Steventon, where Jane Austen had lived as a child, was the smallest and there our Landlords lived in the Manor; it had a tiny Church where we went every Sunday, not on our ponies. Micheldever, from where the Highwayman Michael de Vere had terrorised the travellers between London and Southampton in the 17th century, was a village split in two. The nearest part held the station from which our father caught the London train.

Both Steventon and Micheldever were peaceful havens; when we rode by friendly villagers smiled at us over their front gates, while billowing pillow-cases, shirts and long-johns waved from the washing lines in the back gardens. They each had their village idiot, who wandered about in the middle of the road, scuffing the dust, and slobbering a bit. And they each had a village shop, as in a child's dreams, crammed with tall glass jars full of

"Who d'yer think y'are..."

sticky sweets; as well as postage stamps, loaves of bread, slices of bacon and shelves at the back with neatly folded piles of flannelette night-gowns and stockinet bloomers.

Overton (or Denver) in comparison was a battlefield and there we had to take the ponies to be shod. Straddling the main road like one of the gold-mining towns that Imogen read about in Zane Grey, it had lost a lot of shops, a Garage and industry in the shape of a paper mill, which printed money for the Bank of England.

On the way to the forge we had to ride past the village school, and if the children were in the playground we ran the gauntlet of flying stones and insults. To them it may have been class warfare, but to us it was another skirmish with hostile Indians. The red faces screeched at us, "Yah boo! Bloody toffs! Who d'yer think y'are then, all stuck up on yer bloody pownies?" In my imagination Billy the Kid raked them with his repeater, but in real life we did not deign to reply.

Through traffic would pile up behind us and the ponies begin to fidget and dance about. "Garn then, buck 'er off! Chuck 'er off on the bloody road, yer silly powny!"

The forge was a sanctuary down a little lane at the far end of the village, and once there we tied up the ponies and waited our turn. Mr. Sims was a tiny gnome of a man, who had once been a jockey. It was difficult to hear what he said as he kept all the nails in his mouth, breathing stertorously through them as they stuck out like an extra row of sharp pointed teeth.

The wildest horses calmed down in his presence and soon became very affectionate, nibbling the back of his leather apron as he bent over their hooves or pushing his cap off onto the chalk floor. One of us would run round the corner and buy sugary cream doughnuts and 'Film Fun' or 'Tiger Tim' and sitting on the blacksmith's wall, reading about Lupino Lane and Laurel and Hardy, the battleground at the other end of the village seemed far away.

Mr. Sims was a tiny gnome of a man,

But I never liked Overton. The year before I had had a humiliating experience in the fancy dress class at the fête. Our mother had entered me as the Lady of Shallot and dressed me in a table-cloth pinned at the neck and a home-made conical hat with a white chiffon scarf glued to the top. When the Boy's Brigade Band struck up with a discordant howl at the start of the parade the borrowed pony reared up, and the tablecloth fell off. Things went from bad to worse, everybody laughed and I was eventually given a prize as Lady Godiva.

"What did you expect?" Imogen commented when I got home. "You'd never catch me going in for that sort of thing."

Our father, Marcus, also felt proprietorial rights over the Steventon Estate, at least as far as shooting was concerned. Hand-reared pheasants thronged the coverts waiting for the Autumn slaughter to which he was always invited, being a good shot. Any rabbit or hare that strayed into our garden usually ended up hanging in the game larder. On winter nights in the larch woods, I stood behind him holding my breath: me with my catapult, he with his gun, waiting for the wood pigeons to come to roost.

Sometimes on a Saturday, he would come riding with us. He had an excitable pony called Flash who had been banished from the polo field for being fidgety and highly-strung. Our father having spent the week in London cooped up in his office and Flash idling about in his field, were both in need of physical exercise. Once united a type of nuclear fission took place; our ponies, too, would catch the mood and behave like prancing thoroughbreds.

These weekend rides were different from our daily sorties. They always had to have an objective, which was likely to be a neighbour with a plentiful supply of gin and tonic. It never occurred to our father that our headlong arrival at some friend's door would be other than extremely welcome and despite his daughters' misgivings he was seldom disappointed, the handsome figure that he cut in his whip-cord jodhpurs being almost irresistible.

The Armstrongs at Steventon were particular friends of our parents and occasionally we were sent off to have tea with their three children. It seemed to me a stupid way to spend an afternoon. They lead an orderly life, quite unlike our own, under the strict supervision of their French Mam'selle who gave them proper lessons and hardly ever let them out of her sight.

When they went riding they wore bowler hats and trotted slowly round in a circle in a field. They went for walks down the lanes round the village with Mam'selle pushing John in his pram; they would collect wild flowers and learn their French names and press them into books when they got home. The girls wore dresses with knickers to match. I had to change into a clean pair of shorts for the occasion.

At tea we had to talk French. "La confiture, s'il vous plait," requested Miranda, who was the same age as me, but much larger.

"Le! Le! Le!" screamed Mam'selle, making me jump. "C'est un homme, le confiture! Allez!"

"Oh well, le then," mumbled Miranda, making a face at me where I sat next to her at the round tea table with its tablecloth hand-embroidered with neat little posies of flowers.

"Mais qu'est ce que c'est 'le then', si mal élevée?" Mam'selle's black moustache bristled and the gold crucifix dangling over the front of her blouse bumped up and down.

"Le confiture, s'il vous plait," sighed Miranda, looking up at the ceiling through thick dark eyelashes. My own hair was lank and blonde with almost invisible eyebrows and lashes to go with it, and I felt like a white mouse sitting beside her.

"Voilà."

If we did not ask for what we wanted in French we did not get it. The pot of strawberry jam paused at Miranda and then went on its way round the table. I let it go, not wanting to open that can of worms again. The chocolate cake was a different matter, large and glistening, it had icing in the middle as well as on top.

Imogen was sitting opposite me beside her friend Penelope, with whom she had a much better relationship than I did with Miranda. I stared at her until I caught her eye and filled it with chocolate-cake craving thought-waves.

"Je pense," she smirked at last at Mam'selle. "Je pense que ma petite soeur wants un morceau de gateau."

Mam'selle showed her soft centre, like one of those chocolates that you pick out of a box expecting it to be hard inside and find it filled with scented violet cream.

"Ah, la pauvre petite! Voilà! Voilà!"

The three Armstrongs stared at me. A much larger slice of cake than I meant landed on my plate. Mam'selle's boot button eyes bored into me.

"Alors?"

"Mercy," I replied.

After tea we went down to the drawing room and sat about on the pale pink carpet while Mrs. Armstrong read us a chapter out of the Would-be-Goods. Sometimes Mr. Armstrong would come in wearing a silk dressing gown over his clothes. Next to my father, he was the most handsome man I had ever seen and had the added glamour of always speaking in a husky whisper, the result of having been gassed in the First World War.

Mrs. Armstrong had thin red hair with a kiss curl on one side of her forehead. Her voice was gentle and far away and made me feel sleepy and full of chocolate cake. Round the walls of the room were pastel portraits of the three children looking quite unnaturally charming; Miranda was depicted with a pale blue budgerigar on her finger and a pale pink ribbon in her hair.

On the stroke of six the three children went to bed and if Karin had not fetched us by then we would have to sit stiff with embarrassment as they knelt at the nursery sofa to say their prayers. It did not matter that Penelope was seven years older than John or that John was a boy; they all wore nightdresses and went to bed at the same time.

On the way home Karin let Imogen reach across her and practise changing the gears. Hanging onto the back seat as we lurched along I asked: "Is jam a man in Swedish, Karin?"

"My darling, what can you possibly mean?" As we turned into our drive the car bumped into a pothole and the engine stalled. "Across the gate for third, darling, not sideways; that's reverse."

"Oh, sorry."

"Well, it's a man in French," I told her.

I was fighting my way through an enormous chocolate cake. Budgerigars flew out of it, attacking me, screeching 'le! le! le!' The inside of the cake was warm and sticky, and suffocating. I pushed and pushed at it, but there was no way out. The budgerigars rushed at me, pecking at my eyes and my hair, shaking my shoulder.

"Oh Jane, do stop being such a bore – what are you doing in the airing-cupboard again? Come back to bed." Nobody had told Imogen that you should wake sleepwalkers gently, if at all.

Sometimes we spent an afternoon with the Lanes, who were cousins of the Armstrongs. They lived a few miles away on another estate dear to my father's heart, and where he could also rely on some shooting invitations in the winter. We would ride there on our ponies and have hectic races round the park, leaping fallen trees, with Bridget and Mike whose style of riding was more adventurous than that of their cousins. Then there were peaches and figs to steal out of the immaculate glasshouses and exciting raids on the kitchen garden. The Lanes saw even less of their parents than we did and consequently lived like bandits.

Much as I loved our line of loose boxes and the hoary old tithe barn at home, the Lanes's stable yard was my ideal. In its white wooden tower the stable clock chimed the hours as if the world would never end. A flight of fan-tailed doves clattered up into the sky as we rode in and then settled again to their love-making; the cocks, fan-tails spread and throats trembling with urgent entreaty, pursuing their loved ones along the slate ridges until they all tumbled off at the end.

My pony, Robin, looked very small in his hunter's stall. He put his nose up to the iron bars on the partition and looked at me accusingly.

"You'll be all right," I told him. "I won't be long."

In the rosy-walled kitchen garden we crawled on our tummies under the strawberry nets. The straw round the furry plants tickled our bare arms. Imogen squeezed.

"Sssh!" warned the Lanes.

We were silent, gorging. The strawberries were big and luscious, warm from the sun.

Suddenly the gardener was standing over us, brandishing a pitchfork. "You get out of there, you thieving brats! I'll get yer!"

Under the net we fluttered like trapped blackbirds. Bridget emerged first and stood meekly before the big man idly picking wisps of straw out of her long blonde hair. Aged twelve, she already looked like Veronica Lake and would have softened less stony hearts. "We only took a few, Mr. Furmidge," she drawled.

"Only a few! There's four of you, isn't there? And your Mum wanting them for the party tomorrow night and all! You come along with me, that governess of yours is going to hear about this."

"Oh, please, Mr. Furmidge, don't tell Fraulein!"

"This is once too often, Miss Bridget; this 'as to be put a stop to."

"Why ever do you have such a horrid gardener?" I muttered to Mike as the man marched us down across the shaven lawns to the house. Our own cosy old buffoon, Kilmaster, would never have treated us in this tyrannical fashion.

Unlike the Armstrongs' Mam'selle, the Lanes' Fraulein did not have a soft centre. She went back to Germany at the beginning of the war and we used to fantasise that she had found her true calling as Commandant of a concentration camp. For she liked shutting people up. Her punishment for all of Mike and Bridget's transgressions, great and small, was incarceration.

Oakley was the perfect house for such punishment. All the downstairs rooms had double mahogany doors leading into them, and between the tall doors there was a space of about four feet wide and eight feet high into which no crack of light penetrated. To the German woman these spaces were ready-made prison cells, and into separate ones Mike and Bridget would be thrust and the brass keys turned on either side. It could be several hours before they were let out again, as we knew from experience, for we had often arrived to spend the afternoon only to find one or the other, or both of them, already locked up.

We watched her enclosing them, Bridget's face was very white as the heavy door shut on her. I found Imogen's hand and clung to it.

"Kommen sie, meine kinder, we will have tea now," the Fraulein announced, peering at us through her bifocals and lifting her upper lip to show her yellow teeth. "It is prepared."

"No, no, we've got to go, we can't stay - we said we'd be home early," I blurted out.

We were standing in the hall; with its floor of black and white marble slabs, I felt we were pawns in a game of chess. The Black Queen gestured towards the open door of the schoolroom. She stamped her foot, "Kommen sie! It is prepared!"

Bridget's muffled voice came from between the doors. "Let me out!"

I let go of Imogen's hand and dashed out of the front door and down the steps.

In the stables I flung my arms round Robin's neck. Used to such outbursts of emotion, he turned his head and gave me a friendly nudge.

I had saddled up both ponies by the time Imogen appeared, thoughtfully chewing one of her pigtails. "You shouldn't have run off like that, I thought the old bag would have a fit."

"She'd probably poisoned the sandwiches and wanted us to eat them so she could watch us writhing in our death throes. Will Mike and Bridget die, do you think?"

"Well their parents are coming down by the six o'clock train. There should be enough air in there to last that long."

We galloped most of the way home. Startled rabbits bolted into the hedgerows as we passed, and grey squirrels dashed like wisps of smoke up the trunks of trees. We rounded the turn at the top of the woods knee to knee and then slowed down to go through the gate where the garden began. Inwardly I saluted my shipmates as we walked past the sycamore tree.

There was a reassuring welcome from the dogs in front of the house. Our mother was in the iris garden wearing a floppy straw hat, secateurs in her hand and a trug full of irises at her feet. "Hello, darlings. You're back early. Did you have tea?"

"No. We didn't want to be poisoned."

"Oh?"

"Mike and Bridget were being tortured."

"Now, Jane, you're letting your imagination run away with you again."

We let the ponies out and stood in the field watching them as they rolled luxuriously in the lush grass, grunting with pleasure and waving their legs in the air.

"It's no good telling grown-ups anything," advised Imogen, chewing again. "They never believe you."

"I'm certainly glad we've got Karin for a governess; she's hardly any trouble at all."

Karin was trouble of a different kind. When she had a weekend off she usually went up to London. One Friday I sat on her bed watching her pack her suitcase; she seemed very excited and I was envious that she was going to enjoy herself in a world apart from ours. She wore a black suit with a short jacket and a narrow skirt slightly slit at the side. She turned this way and that in front of the mirror. "Darling, are my stocking seams straight?"

"Yes." She had very long thin legs, and wore high heels for London, which made them even longer.

"Are you sure?" She looked down at them over her shoulder.

"Won't you miss us at all?" I asked.

"But, my darling!" She scooped me up in a hug. She had a lot of scent on. "I am coming back in two days, only two days. Can't I forget about you til then?"

"But what will you do all the time?" London to me was stuffy and noisy, and full of dentists. I followed her down the back stairs, her high heels clicking on the metal treads.

"I shall go shopping, then I shall go to the theatre with a guy, and then we will have dinner and go dancing. But first, I must catch the train." She bent and kissed me. "Goodbye, darling."

On Saturday evening the telephone rang when my parents were having their pre-dinner drinks in the drawing room. I was lying behind the sofa reading a book. My father answered it.

"Hello? Emily, my dear old thing, nice to hear you – what? Hold on, I'll get Myra, there's been a mix up here." He held out the receiver to my mother, covering the mouthpiece as he said in anxious tones, "She wants to speak to Joe."

"Oh, no." Into the receiver my mother said, "Why, Emily, whatever made you think Joe was here? No, … no… he hasn't been here all weekend. We're not expecting him – Emily? Hullo? Hullo?" Turning to my father, "She's rung off."

My father stood wearing his green smoking jacket with his back to the fire, looking like an angry heron. "Bloody hell," he said, throwing his cigarette into the fire. I slid down the back of the sofa.

"What's the matter with Aunt Emily? Has she lost Uncle Joe?"

"Go to bed, you awful child, it's nothing to do with you."

"Yes, darling, go to bed, I'll come up and see you in a minute."

I dawdled on the stairs, straining my ears.

"What an intolerable situation. I need a drink." There was a clink of decanter on glass.

"It's really too bad of Joe, on both counts – and to involve us in this way is so embarrassing. Poor Emily!" My mother's voice was tense with worry.

"I'll murder that girl when she comes back."

"It's not her fault. Besides we don't know for sure…"

"Oh yes we do. We ought to sack her."

"We can't! The children are really fond of her."

My ears began to burn and I ran the rest of the way up the stairs to break the news to Imogen.

I burst into her room; "I say, Karin's kidnapped Uncle Joe," and I told her the story.

"More likely," she drawled, worldly wise, "she's having an affair with him."

"Gosh, what's an affair?"

"Oh, you know, like Tess of the D'Urbevilles."

Imogen read very widely for an eleven-year old; Hardy, Hope, Zane Grey, Dumas, Scott, Kipling and Conan Doyle were devoured avidly. This was useful for me; as when we were riding or picnicking, or at night when I could not sleep she would give me souped-up versions of the plots. When I came to read some of these books later on I found them to be far less exciting than Imogen had made them seem.

I pictured Karin swinging from a gibbet on some windy moor. It was a relief when she returned on Monday wearing a smile as broad as the Milky Way. After a little talk with my mother in the morning room, however, she appeared at lunch with red-rimmed eyes. I knew she should never have gone to that dreary old London.

Chapter Three

Our Father, Marcus, came from an ancient family that settled in North Devon and was the youngest of the ten children of Rear Admiral Sir Edward Chichester, 10th Baronet. At the beginning of our grandmother's fifteen child-bearing years the babies arrived in an orderly procession of girl, boy, girl, boy, girl, boy – their conception marking time with Sir Edward's home leave. Then there came a flurry of three girls in three years and finally, after an unusually long pause of two and a half years, Marcus was born.

With his father away at sea and his three brothers off to boarding school, Marcus's earliest years were spent surrounded by women. The first photographs, however, show that although dressed up in silks and satins, ribbons and bows, in the fashion of the household, he faced the photographer with sleek dark hair and a severe expression in his blue eyes.

Our grandmother and old Nanna were both very strong characters who had tremendous rows about the running of the Nursery, but when Marcus told them to kiss and make up, they did so. He had a restless character and was easily bored and a habit of picking nervously at the end of his fingers which lasted all his life.

"What are we going to do today, what are we going to do today?" he would harangue his sleepy-eyed sisters, sitting up in bed in the mornings.

Mary, Fanny and Joanna, the three girls nearest to him in age, had sharp, unconventional minds. As they grew older the turnover of governesses was more or less continuous. The sisters were possessed with the spirit world from infancy and the maiden ladies of limited means that came to teach them were unnerved by table-turning experiments and the hypnotising of the neighbours' children who came, all unsuspecting, to tea.

"It was quite easy," Aunt Jo told me many years later. "We just stared at them very hard and waved something like a dead mouse backwards and forwards in front of them, and they were gone; deep trance. Sometimes it was quite difficult to bring them back again before it was time for them to go home."

The family seat, Youlston Park, near Barnstaple, was a wonderful place for a boy to grow up in. When he wasn't having lessons with his sisters and their governess, Marcus spent his time bird-nesting in the woods.

As he grew older, his eldest brother Ted's polo mallets were cut-down, and he taught his pony, Nancy, how to play polo.

Ted came back from the relief of Ladysmith a local hero. Sherwell village was hung with bunting and the brass band played him home from the station. Whilst in South Africa he had developed a taste for pyrotechnics and was soon showing Marcus how to wedge sticks of dynamite under the roots of the trees in the park.

It was thrilling to leap on Nancy and gallop away before the explosion shook the ground, sending trunk, branches, leaves and twigs flying into the air. On the lawns round the house the peacocks screamed with fright. There was a serious row next time the Admiral came home on leave.

Then tragedy struck the family. Our grandfather contracted pneumonia while serving in Gibraltar and died, aged fifty-seven. Our heart-broken grandmother sailed out to bring his body home. While she was away members of the other two branches of Chichesters at Hall and Darlington dashed down the long drive in their carriages to loot as much of the furniture and heron-engraved silver as they could carry.

The funeral procession stretched for two miles behind the gun-carriage, drawn by his straw-hatted sailors, on which our grandfather's coffin lay; hundreds of local people lined the route to see the great man pass by, doffing their hats in the shade of the tall scotch firs that lined the Barnstaple Road. He was buried at Sherwell amongst his ancestors and where our intrepid cousin Francis was to find his last resting place many years later.

Our grandparents adored each other. To this day there is a weather vane above the stables at Youlston showing their entwined initials.

Our father's world fell apart. The estate was sold by Ted, the eldest son, who was beginning to develop a fatal attraction for women, three of whom he married, and a penchant for gambling and collecting race-horses and expensive houses in places like London and Brighton. The rest of the family moved to Instow, a dreary seaside resort at the mouth of the Torridge on the North Devon coast. Marcus took as many of his possessions as he could. One was a pet rook, which he carried in a paper bag. While waiting for the train to Instow on Barnstaple station the bottom of the bag, already wet, also fell apart and the bird flew away.

The move from Youlston was the first upheaval in our father's young life.

Our mother's childhood, in comparison, was far more precarious, involving several changes of abode as the family fled her father's creditors. Harvey Jay was a good-looking Irishman with a curly blonde moustache and an extravagant lifestyle, which financially he was quite unable to support. A brilliant horseman, he had taken part in the Jameson Raid in the Boer War and afterwards hunted, played polo, and rode in races. He wrote poetry and dabbled unsuccessfully in farming. He also invested in a series of hare-brained business ventures that soon used up his wife Kate's small inheritance.

Grandfather Jay had usually flown the nest before the bailiffs moved in. Sometimes our grandmother stood her ground and once caused the many duns that thronged the house waiting for her husband's return to wait at table, still wearing their bowler hats. She was a resourceful and philosophical woman and a tower of strength to her five children.

She needed to be, for Harvey was far from being an ideal husband or father. His reappearances from periods of hiding could be quite dramatic. Once, completely drunk after some venture had gone wrong, he decided to walk home along the railway line in the middle of the night. Tripping and falling comatose between the rails, he lay there for several hours while trains passed within inches of his prostrate form.

Our mother, Myra, saw him being carried home on a make-shift stretcher, covered in blood; a terrifying sight for a young child. Various bits of dangling rolling stock had clipped his back but otherwise, amazingly, he was unhurt.

Another time, after concluding a rare successful deal, he bought a double-decker omnibus with two horses and drove it home to Wiltshire. Aged sixteen, his eldest daughter, Judith, was with him and enjoyed standing on the platform at the back repelling would-be boarders. One of the horses broke down badly, but the survivor was turned out on the farm and became the family hack. The bus was occasionally used for carting hay or going to the races, until it, too, was turned out in a field and became an adventure play-ground for the little Jays.

Harvey could be cruel and thoughtless to his children. He forbade Judith, at the age of twenty, to marry the love of her life, even though he was a perfectly suitable young man; some time later she had to settle for second best.

He was always jealous of his only son, George, and sent him away to live with cousins in Canada at the tender age of sixteen. He lavished his affections on the youngest member of the family, ruthlessly transferring them when the next one came along.

Thus Dibby, three years older than Myra, remembered coming downstairs one morning to find him sitting in the hall in front of the fire; "Is that my darling?" he called over his shoulder, without looking round.

"No," replied Dibby. "It's not your darling any more."

Kate had some rich relations, the Belvilles, who kept an eye on the penniless family. Great Aunt Emma was a very kind and generous person who sent much needed money every now and then. Our grandmother had a strong religious faith and a conviction that the Lord would provide, and usually his representatives, the Belvilles, did so in the nick of time. She would even set off down the drive in the dog-cart with the four or five children and their buckets and spades ready for their seaside holiday, confident that they would meet the postman bearing a letter containing Great Aunt Emma's cheque – and they never had to turn back.

To ease the strain on our grandmother and in the custom of the time, the Belvilles took Jane, the prettiest of the daughters, away to live with them in Berkeley Square. She was to grow up in an atmosphere of luxury, quite unlike the life she left behind. There were shopping expeditions to Atkinsons and Aspreys, Harrods and Whiteleys in the Great Aunt's electric brougham. There were balls and theatres to go to, and on Sundays after Church the parade in Hyde Park where the men still wore top hats and morning coats.

Her departure left a gap in the middle of the family and the two youngest, Dibby and Myra, became inseparable. Their education, such as it was, was entrusted to a curious assortment of governesses, some of whom were extremely vicious. One of them tried to teach the girls to play the piano and if they made a mistake would seize them by their hair or by their upper lips and spin them round very fast on the revolving stool.

Our grandmother was in fact musical, and one of her pleasures was to sit at her piano, which she played very well, accompanying her small but charming voice. It was a terrible blow to her when Harvey sold the piano. He was too cowardly to tell her what he had done and hid up a tree in the garden when the men came to fetch it away. Kate was quite used to various tables and chairs and ornaments disappearing to pay his debts, but the loss of the piano was heart-breaking.

Imogen and I never knew our grandfather. After the failure of some last desperate venture he ended his life with a pistol shot, far away from home in a hotel bedroom.

When Myra was sixteen she was sent for a prolonged visit to friends in Northumberland. One weekend Marcus Chichester came to stay. At twenty-five he was already a veteran of both Gallipoli and the Palestine campaign having been commissioned into the Royal North Devon Hussars in 1915. In Palestine his Colonel had been killed beside him and Marcus was wounded in both feet. He had been invalided out of the Army and was now studying for a marine engineering degree at Newcastle.

Myra soon fell in love with this glamorous young man with a limp, but for a while he did not seem to be aware of her existence.

She had been given the job of feeding the hens, which she did every morning wearing a Burberry mackintosh, whatever the weather. With the collar turned up and her short blonde hair, it made her feel like Lilian Gish staggering through a blizzard on the North West Frontier. The big granite house had a long double storey window that lit the great sweep of the staircase within; Myra began to time her crossing of the lawn below, carrying the chicken feed, with that of the languid descent of Marcus, on his way down to breakfast in his dressing-gown, savouring the first cigarette of the day and perhaps glancing out of the window to check the weather.

He became aware of her existence. He took to leaving things behind in the house, such as pyjamas under the pillow, as an excuse to return the following weekend.

Soon the pair were dashing around Northumberland on his motor-bike, Myra holding on tight, wearing a cloche hat with felt grapes over her ears. At the lodgings in Newcastle that Marcus shared with two other young men, this wonderful girl with the long thin arms and legs became known as 'The Paradise Duck'.

Oblivious to what was to be a life-long love affair, Granny Jay sent her daughter to stay with her sister Jane, then married and living in Constantinople. Her Turkey was more peaceful than the one to which Marcus had been despatched as a soldier five years earlier, and for six months Myra almost forgot him. There were picnics on golden beaches, sailing on the Sea of Marmora, parties in the beautiful gardens of the British Embassy and flirtations with the many lonely young officers stationed out there.

On her return she and Marcus became unofficially engaged. In the summer she was presented to the enormous Chichester clan in North Devon, a daunting experience for the young flapper. Some of Marcus's nephews and nieces were almost the same age as she, and all of them looked her over with a critical eye. His mother was an imposing figure with abundant white hair worn in a bun; and the beaky nose, which she had handed down to most of her children. Marcus was her ewe lamb and it was vital that she should approve of his choice of a future wife.

Myra had tea with her mother-in-law to be in her small sitting room, which was cluttered with furniture, ornaments and photographs in the Edwardian style. Marcus went off to play a round of golf at Westward Ho! while the interview took place. Some searching questions were asked about the Jay family's background and Harvey's shenanigans had to be glossed over.

"A businessman, you say, my dear? A successful one I hope?

"Er – quite, I believe."

Then it was the sisters' turn. Still obsessed with astrology, they wanted to know the exact date and hour of her birth, to draw up her horoscope and see whether the stars were propitious.

"So, you're Leo, with Virgo rising," deduced Fan. "Marcus is Aries. Both fire signs. You'll have some terrible squabbles." (She was right; in the first six months of their marriage the couple broke all their wedding china through throwing it at each other.)

"And passionate reconciliations!" added Jo, the romantic dreamer.

"The Egomaniac marries the Prima Donna, to put it bluntly, and Marcus has always managed to get his own way," said Mary.

"I suppose we did spoil him dreadfully as a child," sighed their mother. "He was such a dear little boy."

There were a great many relations to visit. One of them was Francis, the famous aviator, navigator and later, single-handed yachtsman. He was living alone nearby in a cottage overlooking the sea, recovering from the near-fatal crash when he had flown his aeroplane into some telephone wires in Japan on his record-breaking flight from Australia to England. His nerves were in a terrible state, and he had grown a beard to hide behind. During their first meeting, he sat and stared at Myra for half an hour without speaking. Later they became good friends and Marcus was to be best man at Francis's wedding.

Our parents' wedding took place at the Savoy Chapel, an unusual choice of venue, as it was one of the only churches in London where divorcees could get married. There was to be no divorce, no second time round. They were together for the next fifty-nine years.

At one time in their early married life, my father was going on a business trip to Paris; Myra was found sobbing helplessly at Victoria Station as the train steamed out.

"You poor dear! Is he going away for a long time?" someone asked solicitously.

"Yes! Two nights!" she hiccupped.

As D'Arcy Collis remarked many years later, Myra was perhaps her husband's shadow, but she would not have wanted it any other way.

Chapter Four

Occasionally, I was reluctantly prised out of my beloved home environment and sent off to stay with relations on both sides of the family. Of the Chichester Aunts, Fan, two up from Marcus, was my favourite; life with her was full of surprises. From an early age she treated me as a grown-up, and I was fascinated by her accounts of the spirit world, the astral in which she seemed to spend so much time and the Summerlands to which we could all hope to repair after death. From there, while drifting about in endless sunshine, we would be able to communicate with anyone left behind on earth through mediums and automatic writing. I couldn't wait. When I sleep-walked she reassured me that I was only working out my Karma and in my next reincarnation I would be free of that particular affliction.

In her forties, she had married a seriously unbalanced artist called Pat Campbell, but she also had a romantic past. Twenty years earlier she had had an affair with a member of the Russian Embassy in London and given birth to a son. There was no way that my grandmother Chichester would have accepted an illegitimate half-Russian baby, so when she found she was pregnant Aunt Fan disappeared abroad. No-one ever knew where she went. When the boy was born she handed him over for adoption and never saw him again.

A post-script to this story is my own. While waiting for a plane at Bordeaux airport in 1950, I was accosted by a man, probably in his thirties, wearing a black beret. He had noticed my name on my suitcase and asked if I was related to Fan Chichester.

"Yes," I said. "She is my Aunt. Do you know her?"

"No," he replied, "but she is my mother," and moved off through the crowd. Although I always had a close relationship with my Aunt, I never mentioned this encounter to her.

Uncle Pat,... was painting away,

She and Uncle Pat had a daughter, Fiona, who was about my age. When I stayed with them we took turns galloping her pony along the sands at Westward Ho! And we went to tea with Aunt Mary at Instow to collect the latest copy of Prediction magazine, which was handed round among the sisters. Aunt Mary opened the door of her little house on the street and immediately shut it again. When she finally let us in, she apologised. She had a long page boy bob stained with nicotine at the bottom, for she was a chain smoker and usually talked with a cigarette hanging sideways out of her mouth.

"I'm sorry, dears," she said in her deep, smoky voice. "Y'see, I was expecting a red-haired young man with a beard who was going to bring me news from afar. Who's this, Jane? You look just like y'father. Come on in."

Aunt Jo was the youngest sister and although she was the prettiest, her modified Chichester beak set off by corn-coloured hair when young, she never married. She was to be the cause and victim of the terrible scene that took place during my visit.

One morning Uncle Pat decided to paint my portrait. His easel was set up near the window of the big sitting room, out of which the staircase led up to the first floor. At the bottom of the stairs stood a large cow-bell, which was used for summoning the household to meals, although it seemed to me that a shout would have done just as well. In a corner Fiona, my cousin, was playing with her collection of toy horses, which all had real manes and tails you could brush, harness that did up with real buckles, and a tiny wooden stable block to put them away in.

From my reluctant position as the artist's model, I watched her out of the corner of my eye, wishing I could change places with her. In front of me Uncle Pat, with his back to the window, was painting away, taking the deep gasping breaths of a man in the throes of creative labour. He was very short and very fat, and took little darting steps at the canvas, which he stabbed with a long-handled brush. I was terrified of him.

The front door opened and my Aunt Jo and cousin Bimmy came in and made themselves at home, continuing the conversation that they had been having before. There was always plenty of gossip to be had among the relations in North Devon, and they were soon shrieking with laughter and cries of disbelief at each other's revelations. Uncle Pat's breathing grew more and more stertorous and I watched in alarm as his nostrils dilated with suppressed rage.

At last he could stand it no longer. "Women!" he howled, sending the palette and brush spinning to the floor. "Stop your cackling! How's a man to work with your endless cackling?"

Aunt Jo stood up, still laughing. "Sorry, Pat! Where's Fan? We just popped in to see her …"

Fiona, knowing the signs, dashed past them up the stairs. I got off my sitter's throne, uncertain which way to flee. Bimmy beckoned to me and I tucked myself in behind her skirts.

"Just popped in!" roared Uncle Pat, purple in the face. "Can't you see I'm working! Bloody women bursting in!"

"Is she upstairs?" Aunt Jo inquired sweetly and began to climb them herself.

"Oh no you don't," bellowed Uncle Pat. "You don't destroy a morning's work and get away with it just like that!" And seizing the cowbell he pursued her up the stairs, showing great agility for such a short, fat man.

Aunt Fan put her head out of her bedroom as Fiona reached it and pushed her inside. Aunt Jo was not so lucky. As she reached the landing she tripped and fell, and in a minute Uncle Pat was upon her, beating her about the head with the cowbell as she lay at his feet.

I shall always hear the terrible muffled thump it made, while the clapper banged wildly about. At the bottom of the stairs Bimmy was screaming. I clung to her legs. Then Aunt Fan reappeared. "Stop," she said in a loud, firm voice. He did.

Aunt Jo was taken away in an ambulance. Always the vaguest member of the family, after this incident she became distinctly fey and had a dent in the middle of her forehead for the rest of her life.

By the time PC Tudgey arrived to investigate the disturbance, Aunt Fan had shut Uncle Pat up in his bedroom and was standing at the top of the stairs barring the way. The North Devon Constabulary knew all about his violent attacks and wanted to remove him to the local lunatic asylum.

"No cause for alarm, Tudgey," said my Aunt firmly. "My sister just had a little accident."

The policeman shifted from one large boot to the other, took off his helmet and mopped his brow. His superiors would be on at him if something wasn't done soon.

"It's for your own good, Ma'am. You and the little girl would rest easy if the Captain was put away. And you'm be able to visit him Sundays."

But Aunt Fan was adamant. She considered him to be a brilliant artist who was not responsible for his occasional fits of rage.

There was nothing of the supernatural about my mother's side of the family. Old photographs show Aunt Dibby's first husband, Kenneth Leake, to have been very good-looking with keen eyes and slicked back hair, and an empty sleeve where his right arm should have been. He had lost it in the First World War. They are standing together, probably on the day they got engaged. Aunt Dibby is very pretty with curly brown hair, round and radiant as a ripe plum. They look extremely cheerful and ready for a life of married bliss, but this was not to be.

From the start this man stipulated that there should be no children of the marriage, and so when my Aunt conceived her daughter Gilly, he left her.

Later our father was to find her a much better husband, Claud Leggatt, with whom she produced three more daughters and did live happily ever after.

47

These cousins of mine led a less exotic life than those in North Devon and there I was sent to stay, again reluctantly, when Karin went back to Sweden for her annual holiday. They lived in Somerset where villages nestled like eggs in thrushes' nests, reached by narrow twisty lanes between green banks and high hedges. Their house was on the village street, but at the back there was a big garden with a babbling brook, an orchard and the roses, which were my Uncle's passion.

Unlike Kenneth Leake, and Pat Campbell for that matter, he was a very gentle man who, after a career in the navy joined the Imperial Tobacco Company in Bristol, where his long thin nose became expert at sniffing tobacco leaves as well as roses.

From the lawn you could see the hazy blue line of the Mendip Hills in the distance. The Somerset air was warm and sleepy-making.

The Leggatt children had a dreadful Nanny: a tall, thin woman with a pale face, lip-less mouth and dark hair with a widow's peak. She reminded me of the wicked Queen in Snow White. Mealtimes in the nursery were a nightmare. The food was dreadful and whatever the children refused to eat reappeared the next session. Thus, porridge came back for lunch, cold rice pudding for tea, spinach soup for breakfast and so on.

The house had low ceilings and polished wooden stairs that creaked when you ran up them. From the landing you could see the tower of the Church over the garden wall.

I shared a bedroom with Julia who was the same age as me. "Doesn't Aunt Dibby mind about your horrid Nanny and all that beastly food?" I asked when we were in bed. My Aunt seemed to me to be the soul of indulgent motherhood.

"I don't know. Let's have a pillow fight."

We were standing on our beds in the middle of the pitched battle when Nanny burst in, stiff as a board in her starched apron, and brandishing a slipper. A snowstorm of feathers from the exploded pillows drifted slowly from the ceiling, some of them settling on her widow's peak.

With the hysteria of fright, Julia and I got the giggles.

"I'll give you something to laugh about. Come here at once, the pair of you, and bend over." Up went our nightdresses and down came the slipper, very hard on our bare bottoms. We climbed back into bed, rubbing our sore behinds. "Any more of this silly nonsense, and Jane will go straight home in the morning." And she went out, slamming the door.

"I don't mind if I do," I whimpered when she had gone. Nobody had ever hit me in my life.

"Shhh!" admonished Julia.

We had been asleep for about an hour when all hell broke loose. Bing! Bang! Bong! Bing bing bing, bong bong bong, dang dang dang dong! I sat up in bed screaming with terror.

Crash bang! Crash bang! Dang dang dang dong!

"Whatever is it?" I shouted at Julia over the din.

The door burst open and the Nanny rushed in again, a cross between the Wicked Queen and a witch on a broomstick.

"She's frightened of the bells!" screamed Julia before she could wield the slipper again.

As suddenly as it had started, the awful noise stopped. "What a silly fuss, I'm sure. They're very nice bells. Now go to sleep."

"Sorry," whispered Julia when we were alone again. "I forgot to tell you that this is bell-ringing night."

"I wish you had remembered," I was annoyed to find tears pricking my eyelids.

In the morning things got better. Caroline, the youngest, was in her pram, and while the Nanny was hanging out the washing we slipped out of the house and hightailed it down the village street to the shop. This den of goodies more than made up for the disadvantage of living with one of the most famous peals of bells in the West Country over the garden wall.

We stocked up with Mars bars and pear drops, Smith's crisps and Tizer, and hesitated between sherbet with a stick of liquorice poking out of the bag or actual liquorice bootlaces. When we had decided, Mrs. Denby wrote it all down in a little book and hurried into the back room where we could hear a baby screaming.

"Gosh. Don't we have to pay?" I asked as we sashayed off down the village street smoking sugar cigarettes.

"We'll probably settle up at the end of the week when we get our pocket money," Julia was a very pretty little girl, with curly brown hair and I envied her sophistication.

Susan, the younger sister, joined us as we went and lay in the long grass in the orchard, guzzling the spoils. Inside my shorts my stomach began to feel distended with Tizer bubbles and sweets. No wonder the Leggatts never ate their proper food.

The next treat was the recreation ground, an experience quite new to me. It lay at the far end of the village and was a perfect man-made children's battlefield. Stoutly built swings dangled on chains from metal frames, see-saws with hoops to bang on to went round and round as well as up and down, a silver slide soared out of the sky and a big revolving drum with a wooden hedge round it for standing on could be made to go really fast.

The village children were the enemy. Lead by Darlene, the grocer's busty ten-year-old daughter who at other times was to be found meekly measuring out butter beans and lentils behind the counter and was actually quite a good friend of Julia's, they fought us tooth and nail for possession. If one of them was using a swing that we wanted we would wind the jangling chains up tighter and tighter and then suddenly let go, so that the enemy unwound very fast and then fell off. Battles ranged up and down the slide at high speed.

"Charge!" shouted Julia, leading a boarding-party onto the revolving drum. We stopped it in mid-revolution and whizzed it round in the opposite direction. The village children lost their grip and rolled backwards onto the ground. Soon they retreated.

"We'll getcher temorror!" they shouted as they ran away.

"I didn't mind staying with Julia," I confided to Imogen in the saddle-room when we were both safely home again. She had gone happily to stay with other cousins in Gloucestershire. "But I'm never actually going to go away again. Other people's families are not like ours."

"Oh, I am. I'm going to go away to boarding school as soon as I can. Gilly says it's great fun. Besides, I've got to get an education."

"Everything I need to know is here," I said firmly. And taking my tack off its pegs, I went off to catch Robin for a solitary, peaceful ride.

Chapter Five

Our mother was involved in a lot of charities, which was why she had fielded me as the Lady of Shallot in the Overton fête (held in aid of the Church Missionary Society). It was also the reason why we came to have an old lag as a butler for a week. For almost every weekend of that long, hot summer the house had been full of our parents' friends, and by the time Goodwood week came round Mrs. Dowling and the maids were exhausted and showing signs of sullen mutiny.

Hanging around in the loggia one evening as the sunlight faded over the garden and Marcus and Myra drank their cocktails, I heard them discussing the problem. "What we need is a butler. I think I know just the man. The Prisoners' Aid people often find jobs for the prisoners on parole as domestic servants. It's such a lovely change for them and helps them to go straight. The man I'm thinking of actually was a butler before he – well, got into trouble."

"Sounds a bit dubious to me." Our father blew smoke rings into the hazy air as he lay back in one of the long wicker chairs. "Of course, we'd have to lock up the silver. The dining room table would look a bit bare, but if we give everyone enough to drink they probably won't notice." He leaned across with the cocktail shaker to top up our mother's glass.

"I'll ring them up in the morning. I've visited Wilput in his awful East End hostel. I'm sure he'll jump at the chance of a week in the country, and we wouldn't have to pay him very much."

"Is he a rapist? Has he murdered anyone?"

"Of course not, darling, or they wouldn't have let him out. He's just a thief, and not a very clever one at that, which is why he's spent so much time inside. The feeling that we trust him could change his whole outlook on life and, besides, he'd be a great help to Hansi and Bertha who really are looking rather tired."

Percy Wilput did look quite like a butler when he arrived. Kilmaster fetched him from the station and deposited him on the gravel outside the front door. He was wearing a black coat and striped trousers without an arrow in sight, and carried a suitcase too small to conceal more than a couple of salt cellars. With this he stabbed ineffectually at the dogs who, excited by this new arrival, were attacking him from all sides, barking extravagantly and wagging their tails at the same time.

"He seems awfully frightened of them," I commented to Imogen, as we observed him through the window in the apple-loft, high up in the great barn.

"Dogs can tell a shady character a mile away. Mummy must be quite mad."

He came on the Saturday before Goodwood so as to get used to the household. Our parents got used to him and by Monday were behaving as if they had had a butler all their lives.

"Tell Cook we'll be eight for luncheon, Wilput."

"Very good, Madam."

"We'll have coffee in the drawing room, Wilput."

"Very good, Madam."

"Oh, and, Wilput..."

"Yes, Madam?" Etc., etc.

"It's lucky it's only for a week," said Imogen, "otherwise their characters could be permanently ruined."

On Monday morning I watched him cleaning the knives in the pantry, dipping a cork into the pink paste mixture and rubbing it up and down the blades. He was wearing a strange looking apron with a number in the bottom right hand corner – stolen from prison, I assumed.

"It may be Wilput this, and Wilput that to them," he confided, "but you and your sis' can call me Uncle Percy."

"Why?"

"Because we're goin' to be pals, that's why."

A bell tinkled on its curly spring on the wall.

"There she goes again. Some people are never satisfied!"

He whipped a comb out of his pocket, gave his hair a whirl so it stuck up in front in a greasy peak, and went off to deal with our mother.

I peered round the kitchen door. Mrs. Dowling sat at the scrubbed kitchen table with her back to the Aga, pushing some icing sugar through a sieve with a wooden spoon. Although she produced marvellous meals for dozens of people I had never seen her actually cooking anything. The kitchen was always immaculate. On her day off Hansi and Bertha took over and then some very exciting cooking went on, saucepans boiling over, eggs rolling off the table, black smoke coming from the oven and dogs getting into the larder.

Today there was none of that. I sidled in. "It looks awfully lumpy, that icing sugar, Mrs. Dowling."

"What's this, then?" Her beady eyes flew up from the bowl. "You quite made me jump. You know the rule, Miss Jane, 'no children in the kitchen'."

"I just wondered if you wanted any help with that icing sugar, it looks so hard."

"Well, you're a naughty girl, but just this once." She picked out a snowy white lump and put it on the table in front of me.

"Thank you very much." The icing sugar melted like heaven in my mouth. "What do you think of the new butler, Mrs. Dowling?"

"New butler, my foot! If I told you what I thought of him, Miss Jane, your ears would fall off, that's what."

She sniffed and her starched white overall crackled with indignation. I put my elbows up on the table and my hands over my ears to keep them in place.

"It's not a question of like and don't like, it's a question of trust and don't trust, Miss Jane. And I wouldn't trust him with my grandmother's false teeth. The very idea, having a convict in the house."

Bertha came in, pink and blonde. "The table, he lays it all wrong: forks to the right, spoons to the left, all crazy."

Mr. Delitz rushed past the stables being taken for a walk by Robinson

"Maybe he's left handed?" I asked, sticky now with icing sugar.

"He pinched Hansi's bottom with his right hand," observed Bertha.

"Well, there you are!" Mrs. Dowling retorted.

Outside I found Pangloss sitting scratching his glossy black shoulder in his usual place in the shade of the sweet smelling poplar. "Butler my foot!" He looked at me expectantly and thumped his tail on the hard green lawn. I pulled open the Iron Gate and went on up to the stables.

In the saddle-room Imogen was reading 'Sanders of the River' curled up on a pile of rugs. "I'm not going to call him Uncle Percy. I never heard anything so soppy in all my life."

Mr. Delitz rushed past the stables being taken for a walk by Robinson, the pig. Every day he tied a string to one of Robinson's hind legs, and with a strong stick to steer him, set off for the oak tree half way down the drive. He said the exercise and the fallen acorns were good for the pig. The walk usually ended with Robinson turning and bolting for the compost heap in the kitchen garden. There he would rootle for tasty morsels left over from human meals. Today I followed them. I had to run quite fast to keep up.

At the compost heap Mr. Delitz leaned on his stick panting and mopping his brow with a paint-spotted handkerchief. Robinson guzzled away happily at the unsavoury heap, casting over his shoulder anything that did not take his fancy.

"Won't all this dashing about make his bacon rather tough?" I asked.

"It may make the bacon tough, but it makes the old artist tender," Mr. Delitz, rubbed his leg. I wiped away a squashed tomato Robinson had flung at my knee.

Mr. Kilmaster came out of the greenhouse and pushed his green hat to the back of his head, revealing a white forehead like a boiled egg, where the sun never penetrated.

"That old pig, sir!" he wheezed with laughter. "He do lead 'ee a merry dance!" With his pink cheeks and wide nostrils he looked rather like a pig himself.

Mr. Delitz retrieved his spectacles from where they had slipped off his nose. "Now, the problem is to get him to dance back to his sty."

Mr. Kilmaster pulled, I pushed, Mr. Delitz whacked Robinson's bristly back with his stick; eventually with the help of a bucket of swill, he was coaxed home again.

Mr. Delitz was clearly upset that the outing had gone so badly. I followed him into the barn.

"Pigs are very insensitive animals, Jane," he said, sinking into the old armchair. "I shall not take him out again until he has learned some manners."

In their boxes the orphan owls shuffled about on their big feet.

"We've got a butler for a week," I said to change the subject.

"Aha!" he cried, instantly interested. "A butler for a week! How have we existed for so long without one?"

"Mummy's very pleased with him, but Mrs. Dowling hates him, and he's already pinched Hansi's bottom. He's been in prison for being a thief and will probably have stolen everything by the end of the week."

"This is ver' interesting. Your mother has a simple, trusting nature – you can see it in her eyes. Unlike the rest of the world, she does not think the worst of everyone. Every day, little Jane, you must bring Old Delitz a bulletin from the house about this amazing thief/butler."

"I will," I told him, although I was not sure what a bulletin was. It sounded like the stuff that came out of my shipmates' muskets.

By Monday evening the house was full of flowers, the spare beds were all made up and the house party had arrived. The big garage in the barn was full of cars and others stood about on the gravel: big Fords and Bentleys, Rileys and Railtons. The dogs were very excited, using the wheel hubs as lampposts.

The grown-ups had cocktails in the drawing room before dinner and I was allowed to hand round a bowl of nuts, in my dressing gown. I tripped over a small table and the nuts flew out of the bowl, all over the carpet.

"Stupid," said Imogen, helping me to pick them up.

Later we sat on the back stairs, as usual, waiting for the leftovers to come through the serving hatch. There was a terrible lot of clatter in the dining room and the dinner party went on for a long time. Wilput wore a white coat and had combed his hair up into its greasy quiff.

On one of our raids he caught us red-handed, each clutching a chicken leg. "Now then, kiddies! Not so fast! What's your Uncle Percy going to have for supper then?"

"You're not our Uncle Percy and you had your supper before," said Imogen. Sauce from the chicken began to drip down my arm.

"Call sausage and mash 'supper'? No, this is the fare for Uncle Percy. You 'op along to bed, kiddies, and don't let me catch you down 'ere again."

"I hate that butler," said Imogen as we stumped along the passage to our bedrooms empty handed. "I hope he gets a chicken bone stuck in his throat and chokes to death."

Much later, I woke to hear the piano tinkling in the hall below my room. The grown-ups would have rolled up the carpet and be dancing on the parquet floor. Our father would be by far the best looking of the men. I wondered with whom he was dancing. Blue moonlight striped my room as I fell asleep again.

Next day the picnics were loaded into the cars by twelve and the house-party was ready to go off to the races. The women wore little straw hats tilted over one eye and the men had Panamas, double-breasted suits and co-respondent shoes. Someone took a photograph of them all, standing by the front door, blinking in the bright sunlight as the heady scent of jasmine climbing over the porch filled the air.

Car wheels crunched over the gravel. Our parents and some of the others climbed into the Ford V8. It had heavy doors and woollen upholstery that smelled of mothballs.

"Goodbye!"

"Goodbye!"

I waved just as our father slammed the car door. My thumb was caught in it. The pain was excruciating and I screamed. Everybody stopped their cars and got out. My thumb dripped red blood onto the gravel like something out of Struwelpeter. The dogs, Dinah and Pangloss, licked it up.

"Poor darling!"

"Is it broken?"

"Put butter on it!"

"Hurry up, we'll miss the first race."

Our mother led me into the gents, holding my dripping thumb away from her pale green dress. "Put it under the cold tap, darling, that will stop it bleeding. Does it hurt dreadfully?"

"Yes."

"Excuse me, Madam, if you'll pardon the intrusion." Wilput's striped trousers were standing beside me, blurred by my tears.

"What is it, Wilput?"

"May I suggest that you depart as planned to the races, and leave me to deal with the little lady? I have a First Aid box in the pantry to deal with any emergency, which may occur, in the course of duty, you understand."

My mother looked round at him from the basin, her big blue eyes under her little straw hat widening with admiration; as Mr. Delitz had said, she was ready to think the best of everyone. I could feel her wavering. Outside our father was tooting the Ford's melodious horn with impatience.

"Well, if you're sure…"

Toot toot.

"Don't you worry, Madam."

She uttered a few soothing words, kissed the top of my head, and was gone. I heard the last of the cars driving away; I could not believe the duplicity of my relations. I looked at my thumb, dripping redly into the basin. The nail was beginning to turn blue.

Wilput went and fetched his First Aid box and made a good job of disinfecting the thumb and binding it with Elastoplast. Then he sat down on the lavatory seat and looked at me with his rheumy eyes. When he smiled he showed me the curious kind of hinges that held his two sets of false teeth together.

"Well, this isn't 'alf a 'ave and a do. You with your bleeding thumb and me feeling quite weak with the shock of it all. What we want is a drop of medicine to pull us together. Am I right?"

The house was strangely silent around us. I knew that Karin and Imogen were away shopping in Winchester, but Mrs. Dowling and the maids were somewhere about; normally you could hear Hansi and Bertha singing as they dusted and swept, but today there was no sound.

I did not like the idea of medicine at all; perhaps he intended poisoning me before making off with the candlesticks. Our father had forgotten to lock the silver away after all. I followed him into the dining room and there they stood, gleaming in the middle of the table.

"I don't want any medicine. My thumb's feeling much better already."

"Ah. But this medicine's different."

He went over to the big corner cupboard where the drinks were kept and pulled out two bottles. Then he took two glasses out of the sideboard and began to fill them up. His was dark brown and mine was cloudy with froth on top.

"Here's health! Drink up your medicine like a good girl."

"It's not medicine, it's ginger pop and I hate it, it goes up my nose. And that's our father's whisky you're drinking."

Wilput drained his glass and wiped his mouth with the back of his hand.

"Nothing like it for the shock," he filled his glass again. I backed towards the door. His eyes watched me, looking more watery than ever.

"I don't think you should steal our whisky like that! I'm going to tell Mrs. Dowling!" I bolted out of the room and dashed into the kitchen. It was empty, but I found the cook in the larder sorting out the morning's trug of vegetables.

"I'm not surprised," she said mildly, when I had blurted out my story; in fact, she looked almost pleased. "Whatever did they expect?"

"But aren't you going to stop him?"

Mrs. Dowling sniffed. "You won't catch me tangling with an escaped convict," she said. "It's none of my business, I'm sure. You run along now, Miss Jane, and keep that thumb out of trouble."

I dashed through the garden to where my sycamore tree stood, overhanging the dell. *My shipmates looked at me with respect as I was piped aboard.*

"I trust the pain is bearable, sir," said the first mate, eyeing my wound.

I managed a brave smile. "Quite bearable now, thank you, Number One. One cannot expect to survive a battle like that without a few pinpricks. How are the men? Are they in good heart after yesterday's valiant fight?"

"Yes, sir. The wounded have been looked after and the crew were given an extra tot of rum, as you suggested."

"Good."

"There's only one spot of bother, sir."

"Oh?"

"I'm afraid it's Wilput again, sir. Not content with his extra tot, he broke into the store-room and finished off the barrel."

"Hmm. Where is he now?"

"He's in the brig, sir, sleeping it off. I've had him clapped in irons."

"This is grave news, Number One. Have the man brought to my cabin."

"Aye aye sir."

High in my cabin above the swaying leaves I surveyed the surrounding ocean for enemy craft before settling down to the treacle tin of desiccated fudge that I kept there. There was a knock at the door.

"Come in!" I stowed the treacle tin away.

The first mate entered followed by two sailors half-carrying the wretched Wilput between them. His seaman's jersey was torn and he had heavy chains on his wrists and ankles.

"The prisoner, sir," the first mate saluted.

"Well, Wilput," I snarled. "What have you to say for yourself?"

Wilput began to sing in a loud and quavering voice, "For heesh a jolly good fellow, for heesh a cholly good fellow, for heesh..."

"Stop that!" bellowed the first mate. "I'm afraid you won't get much sense out of him, sir, he must have drunk about a gallon of rum."

"Right. Take him below and when he sobers up, give him forty lashes. And make sure that every man-jack aboard witnesses the flogging."

"Aye aye sir."

Wilput leered at me with his watery eyes as he was dragged away.

"God bless you, sir!" he cried. I chose to ignore the man, although a spark of pity touched my heart.

In the morning the real Wilput stood, swaying slightly, on the gravel outside the front door, wearing his bowler hat and carrying his small suitcase. Nobody saw him off when Mr. Kilmaster brought the Austin round and drove him away.

"He's gone." I told Mr. Delitz later.

"Vass?" he cried, holding the wooden spoon with which he had been stirring his porridge up in the air like a conductor's baton. "The butler-for-a-week, he is gone after just a few days? How are we going to manage without him?"

"Much better than with him, I should think. Yesterday after I hurt my thumb he drank a bottle of whisky and Hansi told me that at dinner he poured the gravy down Mrs. Macleod's back instead of onto her plate." We both began to laugh as I warmed to my story. "And then – and then – "

"Yes, yes?"

"He fell over with the fruit salad and broke our best cut glass bowl, and he broke hundreds of other glasses in the pantry. It's like a sort of battlefield in there."

Mr. Delitz took off his glasses and mopped his eyes. "Your poor mother!"

His already high-pitched voice was almost a squeak. "Drink can be a terrible thing, and all this breaking glass is bad for the nerves. You may be right, it is better that he has gone. But what an adventure! Think of the stories he will tell when he goes back to prison. With your golden hair you will be the heroine of Cell Ninety-Three and all the petty thieves in London will want to meet you."

"How do you know it will be Cell Ninety-Three?"

"Well, perhaps Ninety-Two. Anyway, how is your thumb?" He eyed the handsome sling that our father had made for me out of one of his silk scarves.

"It's a little better, thank you."

Actually it was a lot better, the car door had only clipped the top of it, but I was getting a lot of sympathy and milking it for all it was worth.

"Porridge has healing properties, you know," said Mr. Delitz, picking up the wooden spoon again. "Would you like some?"

On Sunday the house party had gone and Mrs. Dowling and the maids had a day off. We had a cold lunch in the loggia. Our father helped himself to cheese and celery and looked across at our mother. "Any more good ideas, darling? How about Jack the Ripper's grandson to come and help in the garden?"

As she lay back in one of the wicker chairs, a band of sunlight fell on her long legs, dressed in pale yellow linen trousers.

"I'm sure Kilmaster can manage perfectly well on his own," she replied coolly. "Anyway, there are no more prisoners available for the time being."

"Thank God for that."

Chapter Six

On my ninth birthday in August I was given a black Pekinese puppy with white paws and a white blob on his chin. Our father brought him down from London in a cardboard box. I picked him up, small and silky, and felt his fine ribcage. He stuck out his tongue and licked my cheek, and I felt as though my heart would break.

"What will you call him?" asked Imogen. She had had her Shetland sheepdog, Bora, for ages.

"Fred." I said, without a second thought.

"That's not a Chinese name!"

"It is now."

"He's got a very long pedigree," our father told us at breakfast, "with all his relations' names on it. I'll show it to you later. Lots of them are champions. You really ought to give him a name like his father's – Poo Kin Chow of Choo Kin Choo, that sort of thing. But you can call him Fred for short; I think it suits him."

I took Fred into the garden and introduced him to the other dogs. They walked round him and sniffed his bottom. I showed him to Hazel and Doris, who squeaked. Fred put his white paws up on the wire of their cage and barked his surprisingly deep-throated bark at them, while wagging his tail furiously. It seemed that the two different ends of him had conflicting personalities.

"It's a boy," said Mr. Delitz, looking at Fred's fat tummy when I held him up for the old man's inspection. "He is very young to leave his mother. You will have to assume the responsibilities of parenthood, little Jane. It is a heavy task."

"I know."

My life changed. I had always been Robin's servant, but I had never been anyone's slave before. Preparing Fred's tiny meals three times a day was a full time job. Cries of "Puddle, Jane! Puddle!" echoed through the house and I would rush for the soda siphon.

"I should call him 'Sure Can Pee'," said Imogen nastily.

In a fortnight Fred was house-trained, but until then my bedroom floor became a sea of old newspapers and comics in case he was taken short in the night. He worried the sheets of paper like a tiger with its prey. In between games he slept fitfully on my bed and snored. I lay awake and watched his small body vibrating with the raucous noise, as loud as an old man in a drunken slumber.

The farmer and his three sons were cutting corn in one of the fields behind the house. Imogen and I, and Hansi and Bertha carried out the tea, as it was too far for the farmer's wife and her daughters to come. There were piles of sandwiches with thick white bread, lots of Mrs. Dowling's fruitcake, and thermoses of pitch black tea. I carried one of the smaller baskets as I was also carrying Fred. The wooden sails of the reapers made a clattering sound as they whirled round and round, flinging the sheaves of corn out sideways. There was a smell of diesel oil and hot straw. Imogen and I helped to make some stooks, and the thistles in the corn scratched our bare arms. When I put Fred down he got lost, as the stubble was above his head, but Dinah, Pangloss and Bora galloped about with their ears flapping, playing games with the farm dogs. Above us white puffs of cloud were almost stationary in the blue sky.

We had tea sitting in the corner of the field. Flies buzzed round the fruitcake and the sweaty men. Hansi had a pink ribbon in her fair hair and was wearing the cotton dress with the tight bodice; she leaned against Harold, the eldest son, while Bertha filled the mugs with tea. The middle brother tickled Fred's snub nose with a straw and made him sneeze. Everybody laughed. The youngest son, Donald, had an awe-inspiring squint. His mouth was always open and he dribbled when he drank his tea; if you spoke to him he turned his head away and tucked it into his shoulder as though he thought you were going to hit him.

The dogs lay in the shade panting, their long pink tongues hanging out of their mouths, watching us eat. Fred sat on my lap and had some cake.

"That was a bit of all right, then," said Mr. Ranger, the farmer, wiping his mouth with the back of his hairy wrist. "Ta very much. Come on boys, back to work; we'll soon have this lot finished."

Reluctantly the sons got to their feet; soon there was only one square block of uncut corn left, standing like a regiment with golden lances in the middle of the field. Harold and his father stopped stooking and came and fetched their guns from under the tree where their lunch satchels were lying. I put Fred in one of the empty baskets and gave him to Hansi to take back to the house. Then I went and stood beside Harold in a corner of the field and loaded my catapult with a pebble.

"You'll never hit nothing with that old catapult," he drawled in his slow Hampshire voice.

"I might."

"Sick 'im! Sick 'im! Go fetch! Fetch 'em out!" shouted the men and the two black and white farm dogs together with ours launched themselves into the corn to bolt the animals hiding there.

A rabbit dashed towards us, zigzagging over stubble and Harold took aim. Its flying body turned a somersault and lay still. Donald and Arthur stood on the tractor banging the metal sides with their hands. More rabbits bolted, stopped, ran on again, turned somersaults and lay still.

Imogen passed behind us, walking up the hedge towards the house. "I'm going. I hate this bit." Her face was red from the sun and she was chewing one of her plaits.

I stayed. I was gripped by the tension of the scene, with the two men standing motionless with their guns at opposite ends of the field and the brave wild animals making a desperate run for it from their dwindling refuge. I held my catapult at the ready, the sling stretched, waiting for something to come near enough for me to let fly.

Then a hare bolted, ears flat on her back, so fast that Harold missed his shot and only wounded her; demented, she dashed round and round in circles, screaming like a baby. I bolted then, too, almost as fast as the hare, back to the garden with my hands over my ears to cut out those dreadful screams.

I caught up with Imogen near the tennis court. "Ah, here's my bloodthirsty little sister."

I uncovered one ear, testing, and the screams had stopped. "It was horrible! A poor hare, and Harold only wounded her."

"Well, he's killed her now. But what about her children left behind in the corn? Just imagine what it's like, hearing the reaper coming nearer and nearer to your home, slashing away at the corn – and you've got to make up your mind whether to save yourself or stay and die with your babies."

"D'you think she had leverets in there?"

"Of course."

In the distance we heard the tractor starting up again and in my mind's eye I could see the flailing sails advancing relentlessly upon the terrified animals.

"Cry baby bunting!" shouted Imogen as I ran the rest of the way back to the house. "Bet you'll have a nightmare tonight!"

I was in the middle of a giant stand of golden corn, the stalks as thick as birch trees. At my feet four Fred-like puppies lay curled around each other, watching me with frightened eyes. I stood listening to the throbbing heartbeat of the reaper as it came gradually closer. The puppies whimpered. 'It's all right, it's all right, trust me, we'll get out somehow.' I picked the puppies up, two under each arm, and lowered my head, trying to batter a way through the corn. A heavy bar blocked my way and over it loomed the huge face of a dog with a milky glass eye.

'Sick 'im! Loo in there! Fetch 'em out!' I heard the farmer's voice shouting. The puppies began to scream with terror. There was a loud crash as the glass-eyed dog lunged at us.

"Well, whatever have we here?" asked Mrs. Dowling, switching on the light in the larder. "Why, it's Miss Jane – and look at all this broken glass.

Whatever do you think you're doing? If you wanted a drink of milk you only had to ask. I'll fetch Miss Sandberg."

Every Sunday we went to the little Church at Steventon where Jane Austen had worshipped as a child. We always sat in the second pew, behind the Hutton Crofts and in front of the Armstrongs. The Hutton Crofts were an elderly childless couple who lived at Steventon Manor, owned the estate and were our landlords.

The Armstrongs were usually the last in, although they lived just across the road in the Rectory. Miranda always managed to sit just behind me. Her parents, wrapped up in their devotions, were oblivious to the pitched battle that ensued. When I sat back in the pew Miranda would tip my hat, felt in winter, straw in summer, and a source of loathing to me, over my eyes. When I knelt down to pray she pushed screwed up sweet papers down the back of my neck. When we stood up to sing a hymn I turned round and stuck my tongue out at her.

"Jane darling, do behave," whispered our mother. From behind I could hear Miranda's treble piping sweetly and wondered what she was planning next.

The sermon was the high point of the service. Rev. Hall, the parson, was a man with a grudge against the upper classes who used his half hour slot to give it an airing. From the pulpit he glared down at his captive audience. Those few of the village people who came to Church sat at the back, well out of reach of his wrath.

The Hutton Crofts, in the front pew, were a soft target.

"Is it not written?" screamed Rev. Hall, gripping the edges of the pulpit till his knuckles whitened. "Is it not written that it is easier for a camel to pass through the eye of a needle than for a rich man to enter the Kingdom of Heaven? Where will you be, Colonel, when the Day of Judgement comes? Roasting in the flames of Hell, that's where."

Colonel Hutton Croft, whose thoughts had been far away, would shift uneasily on the embroidered pew liner, fold his arms and stare fixedly at the

Rev. Hall, the parson, was a man with a
grudge against the upper classes

beams of dusty sunlight slanting through the Austen family's memorial window. Every week he wrote a letter to the Bishop of Winchester, urging him to replace the raving incumbent of Steventon Parish Church.

"And as for you, Lady Barstow!" We children stared across the aisle as the parson's new victim started awake at the sound of her name and adjusted her lorgnettes.

"Surround yourself with good works and charitable fiddle-faddle as you may, the Good Lord can see through to your inner wickedness. I've seen you! But that doesn't stop you turning your cowman out of his cottage at a moment's notice, and he a family man with six children to support. Oh, the flames of hell will have a lovely time with you, Lady Barstow, so they will. And now to God the Father, God the Son and God the Holy Ghost, and may the words of my mouth always find favour in Thy sight, Merciful Lord."

"Eh? What's that?" inquired Lady Barstow.

The parson seemed to leave his class prejudices behind in the pulpit. After the Service he stood in the porch to shake us all warmly by the hand, and did not hesitate to accept his weekly invitation to drink a glass of sherry at the Manor. Our parents and the Armstrongs were usually invited as well.

The lawn of the Elizabethan Manor House was enclosed by a rosy brick wall against which grew roses and espaliered peach and pear trees; while the grown-ups sipped sherry inside the house, we children were left to play on the lawn and eat as many peaches as we liked.

I found a really unripe peach and aimed it at Miranda. I missed; she caught it, threw it back and hit me on the forehead.

"I hate peaches," said Imogen. "The skin sets my teeth on edge."

"So do I," agreed Penelope. "It's like the green baize on billiard tables."

"Exactly," they wandered off together, bored, sophisticated twelve-year-olds.

Miranda and I got hold of each other's hats and jumped on them.

We found some ripe peaches, warm from the sun, and lay on the grass eating them and spitting the stones at each other.

"Is it not written?" screeched Miranda suddenly, shaking her fist at the sky. "Is it not written that it is easier for a camel to pass through the eye of a needle than for a greedy girl called Jane to enter the Kingdom of Heaven?"

We rolled about on the beautifully mown grass and fought like puppies.

"What a charming girl that Miranda is turning out to be," observed my mother in the car going home.

"She's not very charming if you sit in front of her in Church."

Chapter Seven

The summer was drawing to an end. The fields were bare and bristly now the corn had gone, and Imogen and I raced each other on our ponies over the stubble. In the woods thin young pheasants with half grown tails huddled together in clearings looking for their friend, the keeper, to come and feed them; sometimes you came upon a group of them standing in a lane, like people waiting for a bus. Partridges called to one another in the faint blue mist that hung, like a chiffon scarf, over the land in the evenings.

Our father bought a new gundog for the coming shooting season, a liver and white spaniel called Sam, as Pangloss with his grey muzzle was too old, and Dinah too young and silly. Sam was sent away to be trained, and after a fortnight we went to see how he was getting on. The old keeper who was training him had no roof to his mouth, or so his extraordinary way of speaking was explained to me. He took us and Sam out into a field near his cottage and flung the dead pheasant he had brought with him as far as he could. The bird hit the ground with a thump.

"Ham!" shouted the keeper, "ho hetch! Hey yoss! Ham, Ham, ho hetch!"

Sam wagged his tail in a frenzy of excitement, his whole fat body shaking, and then put his paws up on the old man's shoulders and covered his face with kisses. The keeper wiped his chin on his sleeve, retrieved the bird and repeated the exercise.

"Hood hog. Ham! Ho hetch!"

Again Sam smothered the keeper with love.

"Hmm," said my father pensively, rubbing his own chin. "Try something else. Will he come to heel?"

"Ho, hes. Hery hood hobedient hog."

We walked a little way down the field with Sam floundering around us still wagging his whole rear end.

"Heel, Ham," commanded the keeper, tapping his boot with his stick. "Hood hog, Ham, heel."

Sam sped away across the grass, picked up the pheasant, which was still lying there and brought it back, dropped it at the keeper's feet and put his paws back on the old man's shoulders.

Our father puffed at his pipe. "I expect it's only a question of time. He's just got the commands muddled up."

We paid off the keeper and took Sam home. It wasn't a question of time, unfortunately; in all the years Sam lived with us he remained an amiable fool, never learning the difference between a heel and a dead pheasant. He was quite good at blundering through brambles, bolting rabbits around the farm, but when our father was invited to the big winter shoots on neighbouring estates he was left at home.

The changing seasons had no effect on Number Five, Railway Cottages, where Vince, the odd-job man, lived with his mother. The cottage was at the end of the row built beside the long tunnel over the London line and no light penetrated the tiny, net curtain shrouded windows. Inside it was as dark and musty as a rabbit hole. Old Mrs. Vince was crippled with arthritis, and in the early mornings, before he walked across the field to work for us, Vince would build up the fire in the range and settle her in front of it in her armchair to wait for him to come home again. All day long she sat before the fire like a little old hunch-backed rabbit, occasionally riddling it with the poker left within her reach.

"Aren't you afraid she'll fall in?" I asked as I stood outside in the bright September sunshine watching Vince splitting kindling with the dexterity of someone slicing butter with a hot knife.

He pulled the butt of a cigarette out from his tobacco-stained moustache and threw it into the cabbage patch.

" 'Er won't fall! 'Er's all right, 'er listens to the trains."

Inside the cottage your eyes soon got used to the dim light. I liked to look at the yellowing photographs, framed in passe-partout hanging on the rose-patterned wallpapered walls, of Vince and his two brothers. In their ill-fitting uniforms, they stood in heroic attitudes in the photographer's studio, about to go off and fight, and in the case of the two brothers, die, in the First World War.

" 'Ere's Miss Jane come to see us!" shouted Vince into his mother's ear. Beside her on a little table stood a large alarm clock with a luminous face and heavy tick.

"The eleven thirty were six minutes late today," said the old woman in a voice like a pin scratching on slate.

"That's right, Mother! You keep a watch on them trains! Maybe 'er'll be early tomorrow!"

Vince winked at me and took the kettle off to fill it at the tap outside the back door.

"Never 'as been, not since I've been yere," squeaked Mrs. Vince. "And that's eighty-seven years!"

It was an unimaginable length of time to me and I did not know what comment to make. I stared at the photograph of the young, clean-shaven Vince leaning negligently against a broken pillar. In the background smoke seemed to drift across some battlefield. There was something terribly sad about Vince's legs in his boots and puttees, and even sadder about those of his brothers, which carried their owners off to war and did not return.

The kettle took a long time to boil on top of the range and the tea, when Vince made it, a long time to stew in its earthenware pot. Until it was ready we played dominoes. I made a little wall of mine, facing inwards, but Vince and his mother held them expertly in their hands, spread like fans. The old woman's knobbly fingers often let the dominoes slip and when this happened I had to crawl under the table to recover them.

"Don't you go looking at them, dearie! Your girl-friend's cheating again, Charlie!"

"No really, I'm not." It was difficult enough to see the little white dots on the dominoes on the table, let alone those under it.

"She never, Mother. You mustn't say such things to our Miss Jane."

After that I put the dominoes back in their box and we had our tea

I put down a double six sideways and Vince moved the broken match in my side of the cribbage board up to the end and round the corner.

"There she goes! Cheating again!"

The budgerigar in its cage by the window rang its bell, as if to herald the London train that rumbled underneath us through the tunnel.

Mrs. Vince snatched up the clock and held it to her nose, letting her dominoes fall again. Just as Vince was pouring out the tea our cups and saucers began to jump about with the vibration.

"That'll be the four-twenty, regular as clock-work." Mrs. Vince put the clock down and swivelled towards me in her chair. With her beady eyes almost level with the table it seemed to me that she could be the one who was cheating.

"Right, dearie, your shuffle and Charlie's drop."

I had to stand up to shuffle the pile of black bricks. One of them fell over, exposing its underside.

"There she goes again! You'll 'ave to watch 'er, Charlie!" This time Mrs. Vince began to laugh, a sound like a very old pair of bellows with dry leather between their wooden sides; quite quickly she turned deep purple and the laughter became a choking fit, which threatened to be the end of her. It was quite a long time before the spasms subsided.

After that I put the dominoes back in their box and we had our tea.

As I was leaving, another train roared under the tunnel and I felt the ground shake under my feet. After it had gone a cloud of acrid smoke floated up out of the cutting and enveloped Vince and me as we stood in his back garden. He did not seem to notice the awful stench of it.

"I 'ope 'er's on time. Mother'll be after 'er if 'er ain't!"

"Thank you very much for tea, Sir Charles," I said, when we could see each other again.

"My pleasure, Your Ladyship," and he doffed his cap in a mock bow.

I walked across the long field that separated our house from the railway cottages.

While I was giving the guinea pigs their supper, I heard a train rumbling in the distance and saw again the scene in the tiny dark kitchen, the cups rattling on their saucers and old Mrs. Vince checking the clock. I was glad of our airy white house with its solid foundations.

Imogen and I rode our ponies down through the early morning mist to a forbidden field near Steventon to gather mushrooms. Cobwebs beaded with dew were slung between the blades of grass, making a shining net over the field where the sun slanted. In the larch woods, pigeons called to each other - 'Take two cows, Taffy, take two' - as we tied the ponies to the gate and spread out across the field. Our boots and trousers were soon soaking wet from the dew-drenched grass. Trespassing was exciting and we did not speak; the tenant who farmed this land for the Hutton Crofts was an ugly man with a quick temper to match his looks and he did not like finding children and ponies in his field. He would shake his stick at us and threaten us with prosecutions, whatever they were.

Today we struck lucky. Neither the farmer nor the gypsies that sometimes stripped the field in the dawn were around and we soon found the secret clusters of shiny white mushrooms, their tops straggled with the grass they had pushed through during the night.

We picked so many there were some left over for Mr. Delitz. After a breakfast of bacon and mushrooms and fried bread, I took a bag-full to him in the barn. I was surprised to find him making huge unruly bundles of his belongings, tying them up with string.

The place looked desolate. The big umbrella, the easel, the tin bath, the campstool and the screen were leaning against the wall. The bed was bare to its springs. The Primus stove was in a cardboard box with Heinz Baked Beans written on the side.

"Mr. Delitz! You're not leaving already?"

The old man straightened up and pushed his spectacles back up his nose. A big bundle leant against his legs. "Vat is this *already*? Already I have stayed too long. Already the swallows have gone South and old Delitz is still here. The winter is coming, little Jane, and I must go back to work."

"To London?"

"To London. But like the swallows I will come back in the spring, if your mother will have me."

"Of course she will." I felt very sad, the spring seemed a hundred years away.

He bent over the bundle again. "Now, if you will put your little pink finger here, I will be able to tie this stupid knot. There is no time to be lost, Alex is coming to fetch me at eleven."

I lent him my finger and then went and sat in the old armchair, which I knew was staying as it belonged to us, and watched him while he finished his packing. I hoped Alex, his son, had a big car. Grimy saucepans and frying pans, spoons and forks, and plates and mugs disappeared into an old pillowcase.

Fred waddled about sniffing the smelly boxes where the baby owls, long since fledged and flown away, had started their lives. I remembered them, fluffed up in their furry down in the spring opening their beaks in their old, old faces to receive their daily dollop of porridge.

I felt that part of my life was going away. "I hate the summer ending."

"Partir, c'est mourir un peu!" said the old man, packing paint tubes into a box. "But you have the whole of your life before you, little Jane! There will be many more summers, many more springs, many more winters to look forward to." He took off his spectacles and rubbed them with a big red handkerchief.

Suddenly I remembered the bag of mushrooms I was still holding. "I brought you these, but there doesn't seem much point in them now."

He looked inside. "They are beautiful! So white! So pink underneath. Never shall they be eaten. I will paint a beautiful picture of them and send it to you. Which reminds me. I have something for you as well."

He opened a big portfolio, which had not been made into a bundle and took out a little pen and wash drawing of Fred, lying asleep on the lawn.

On the back was written 'A Mademoiselle Jane, un souvenir de l'été, 1938. Leo S. Delitz.'

"It's perfect. Thank you very much." I kissed his bristly cheek. "I'll treasure it forever." I was particularly proud of the grown-up French dedication.

Fred came over and sniffed it.

"He will become very conceited now he is an artist's model," said Mr. Delitz.

"He already is."

At eleven Alex rattled and banged up the drive in a little car about the size and shape of one of his father's bundles, now lying in a heap outside the front door. I picked up Fred and held him against my cheek while the other dogs clustered round, barking.

Alex was tall and thin and already going a little bald like his father. It took a long time to pack Mr. Delitz's summer into the car, and even then it was only half inside: the big umbrella and the legs of the easel had to stick out of one of the back windows.

Our mother came to say goodbye.

"Thank you, Myra, for everything. You are a wonderful woman," Mr. Delitz kissed her hand.

"We shall miss you, Leo, come back next year. And give my love to Fritzi."

Fritzi was Mr. Delitz's long-suffering wife who worked as a midwife in a very poor part of London, and, as our mother had told me, was the only one of the family who earned any real money.

"In January I may have an exhibition of my summer collection." Mr. Delitz put on a dark blue beret that I had not seen before and pushed his spectacles back up his nose. "You must all come and see what a wonderful artist you have had living in your barn."

"Of course we will."

"Goodbye, little Jane." He kissed me and patted Fred on the head.

"When I come back he will be a big dog, a real Chinese dragon."

Then they were gone, leaving only a smell of dirty exhaust fumes hanging on the air of the drive. Soon that was gone, too.

Our mother put her arm round my shoulders. "Let's go and pick sweet peas." We walked up through the wrought iron gate to the flower garden.

It was many weeks before I could make myself go into Mr. Delitz's part of the barn again.

Chapter Eight

There were to be some more departures that autumn. One afternoon returning from a ride I found Robinson, the pig, lying in the wheelbarrow behind the stables with all his trotters in the air, stiff as an upended wooden table. His throat had been cut and he smelled horribly of burned hair: Mr. Kilmaster had been singing his bristles. Robin shied, pivoted on his hind legs and bolted back across the field, I clung to his thick black mane and just managed to stay on.

It was an undignified end for Robinson, but I was not really sorry for he was an unlikeable character and had a nasty way of diving through your legs when you took him a bucket of swill. For several days afterwards varied dismembered bits of him stood in the larder, and Mrs. Dowling was busy making brawn and salting hams. Yards and yards of chitlings were hung up in the boiler room to dry, before being carried home across the fields by the Kilmasters. I wondered what Mrs. Kilmaster did with them; perhaps she knitted them into the curious garments that her husband wore when he was gardening.

The news of the next departure came as a bombshell. At lunch one day there was a funny atmosphere in the dining room as though something were about to happen. Nobody talked very much and our mother and Karin kept exchanging glances. Then our mother ate up the last of the cottage pie and announced: "Karin's got some exciting news for you, darlings; she's engaged to be married!"

Engaged to be married! Imogen and I both looked at Karin in alarm. Her eyes were side open and slightly swimmy, and she certainly looked very excited. Imogen burst into tears. "You can't!" She and Karin were great friends. I watched as Karin put her arms round her and hugged her, almost crying herself.

"Darling, I am so happy! Be happy for me!"

"Who is it?" I asked sternly. I, too, felt betrayed, but I wasn't going to cry.

"It is a wonderful, beautiful man; he is a pilot in the air force. You will meet him this evening. Your kind Mummy has asked him to dinner."

"You can't leave us!" sobbed Imogen.

"She won't have to, they can both come and live here, can't they, Mummy?"

"I think when Karin is married she and her husband will want a home of their own, darling,"

I could just see it, a little cottage near an airfield with check curtains blowing in the windows and dozens of little blonde children running in an out. It was awful. They would be far away and perfectly happy.

"But what about us?" Imogen gave a loud sniff and ran out of the room; we could hear her feet clumping up the stairs.

Her bedroom door slammed.

"Excuse me, Myra," Karin made a gesture of happy despair and followed her.

There was silence in the dining room. Then, in the corner under the window where the dogs were lying, Fred began to snore; his chin was propped up on one of Dinah's paws.

"Oh dear," said our mother, getting up and beginning to pass the plates through the hatch to Hansi. "Imogen is so very emotional."

"So am I. Where did she meet him? I don't see how she went and got engaged to be married without us knowing anything about it."

"You must remember that we are only a part of Karin's life; she has lots of friends and she probably met him on one of her weekends in London. Pudding?"

I would have liked to have been too emotional to eat, but then I saw the treacle tart, a confection, which in Mrs. Dowling's hands was irresistible.

"Well, just a little bit."

The pilot arrived romantically out of a blazing sunset not in an aeroplane, but in a bright red two-seater car. He was a bit smaller than Karin and had very well brushed sleek brown hair with a middle parting. I watched out of the side of my bedroom window as Karin kissed him and took him off for a walk round the garden.

Imogen was allowed to stay up for dinner, she came into my room wearing a dress that had fitted her in the summer. I stood on my bed to do up the reluctant zip. Her eyes were still red from crying in the afternoon. "We've got to put a stop to this, we'll have to put her off him somehow. She's part of our family now."

Downstairs in the drawing room, in my dressing gown, I watched the pilot closely. He seemed very nervous. He tripped over one of the dogs and upset an ashtray. Our father, looking serene and handsome in his dark green velvet smoking jacket, opened a bottle of champagne and we all drank the health of the happy pair; the bubbles in my small glass went up my nose.

When it was time for me to go to bed Karin picked me up in her arms and carried me upstairs, although I was too big for that sort of thing. She was wearing a narrow black dress and had to take tiny steps on the stairs, but when we got to the landing she did a little dance, whirling me round and round humming at the same time. One of my slippers fell off.

She bounced me into bed and bent over and kissed me. "What do you think of him, darling? Isn't he wonderful? Isn't he beautiful?"

"Yes, he is, quite."

"Goodnight, my darling, happy dreams." She turned off the light and went out.

I was almost asleep when Imogen came in. "I've brought you some pudding," she said, and sat down on my bed. Fred woke up and licked some crème brulée off my finger.

"What's he like?" I asked.

"All right, I'm afraid. In fact, it's rather a difficult situation. They are obviously very deeply in love."

The very thought made the back of my neck tingle. I lay back on the pillow. "Are you sure?"

"Yes, and Mummy and Daddy like him, too. I'm afraid there's nothing we can do; we'll just have to let it happen."

Karin was to be married in Sweden, and all too soon the time came for her to leave. To cheer us up and as a final treat, she proposed taking us to the cinema in Winchester one Saturday afternoon. Imogen was against me being included in the excursion.

"It'll be too much for her," she grumbled. "She's only been to one film in her life and that was 'Susannah of the Mounties'. Besides, she'll be sick in the car."

"I won't! I won't! I won't be sick in the car, and if there are any frightening bits, I'll hide my eyes."

"And so will I," Karin laughed.

"Please let me come!"

"I won't take any responsibility for you," Imogen declared haughtily.

"The responsibility will be all mine," said Karin. "I hope you won't be too ashamed of us, Imogen."

The Regal Cinema in Winchester was a revelation to me. An illuminated electric organ entertained us before the film began, I sat back in my dusty red plush seat and stared at the scantily dressed ladies who decorated the proscenium arch, each holding what looked like a giant ice-cream cone from which tumbled a great many apples and pears. Acres of shimmering gold curtain covered the screen, while the organist plucked at our heartstrings with sentimental tunes. I felt as if I were participating in a scene from my book 'The Arabian Nights' – a view not shared by the rest of the Saturday afternoon audience.

Winchester children seemed to take the cinema in their stride and amused themselves by munching sweets, throwing various missiles at each other and clambering over the backs of the seats. For me, however, it was a magical experience; outside entertainment, except for perhaps a pantomime at Christmas, which I hated, played a very small part in our lives.

"Here we go, darling," said Karin, patting my hand on the arm of the seat as the billowing gold curtains parted and 'The Drum' began. It was a stirring film that immediately engrossed me. I identified myself with Sabu and his heroic attempts to save the British Army from certain disaster.

Given the circumstances, I felt I would have behaved exactly as he did, even if my face was the wrong colour.

In the interval, Karin smoked and we had a choc-bar. "All right, darling?"

"Yes, thank you; more than all right," which was true at the time. The mistake we made, as far as I was concerned, was staying for the second film.

'The Terror' was to change my whole attitude to cinema and haunt me for many years to come. Deep in the bowels of some dreadful old castle, hung about with cobwebs and instruments of torture, a mad monk also played the organ, but rather differently from the cinema organist. His music was the music of the devil, and he accompanied it with a burst of maniacal laughter. The black cowl of his habit flopped over his face and there were close-ups of his hands on the keys clad in long, black, pointed gloves. I slid down in my seat and clung to Karin.

The scene moved to the enormous drawing room upstairs in the castle, where a collection of irritable grown-ups in evening dress walked about waiting for their dinner, their faces shadowy in the flickering firelight. Wax dripped from huge candles in creepy sconces against the walls. One of the ladies strayed near a window; through the curtains came the long, pointed gloves of the mad monk to grab her round the neck. She screamed and so did I. I saw the rest of the film in tiny strips through Karin's fingers; I held my own hands over my ears to cut out the spooky music and crazy laughter as the mad monk did away with one elegantly dressed victim after another. I think he was garrotted in the end by one of his own instruments of torture, but by then I did not really care.

It was almost dark when we came out, the evening star twinkling in a lavender sky above the bustling town. It was a relief to find life going on in a normal way after our experiences in the mad monk's castle. I climbed into the back seat of our big Ford and we started on the long drive home. In the front, Imogen and Karin animatedly discussed the beastly film, their faces eerily lit up by the illuminated dashboard.

We had not gone many miles before I felt the familiar knot forming in my diaphragm. I opened a window and breathed in the fresh air.

"What's that draught?" asked Imogen, turning round. "It's freezing cold. Oh Lord, I suppose you're going to be sick."

The old salt taste filled my mouth, my stomach's final warning.

"Yes! Karin, stop the car, please! Just for a minute."

The car drew into the side of the road and the headlights whitened the grass verge and the trees beyond. I wrenched open the door and bolted into the wood, throwing up behind a bush.

"All right, darling?" asked Karin sympathetically, when I trotted back. "Better now?"

I was trying to find my way down a long dark passage, which I knew lead to the moat and freedom. Cobwebs brushed my face as I crept along and I could hear the shuffling footsteps and heavy breathing of the mad monk, following me, gaining on me. I began to run, the stonewalls of the passage crumbling where I grabbed at them with my hands. There was a light at the far end, I was nearly there, just a few more yards; suddenly the monk was standing in front of me, his arms outstretched, barring my way. I could see his ghastly white face and grinning mouth inside the black cowl and now his fingers in their long black pointed gloves reached for my throat. I clawed at his habit, trying to push past him, trying to escape those awful fingers, but his arms closed round my shoulders and Karin was hugging me tightly, my face pressed against her bosom in the black dress that she was wearing for dinner.

Karin carried me back to bed and stayed with me for a long time that night. In the summer we had been reading a Swedish book, 'The Wonderful Adventures of Nils' and now we reached the last chapter. Osa, the goose-girl and her brother, little Mats, find the tiny wooden shoe that has fallen off Nils's foot as he flew, on the back of the wild goose who has adopted him, over the snow-dusted forests. They read his name inside the shoe and knew that he was safe, even if he had turned into an elf. It is a deeply satisfying story.

Karin shut the book. In spite of myself I felt sleepy. "What will I do when you're not here any more? Nobody else knows how to wake me from sleep-walking."

"I don't know, my darling, but if you must sleep-walk, try the airing cupboards again. The cellar with all those steps and dusty passages is much too dangerous. Besides, your father might get the idea that you've taken to the bottle!"

Chapter Nine

Imogen was the next to leave, although her absence would only be temporary: three months incarceration in a boarding school, in south Devon. She had always wanted to go to boarding school and now she was off, to join her cousin Gilly in an establishment near Budleigh Salterton.

She appeared after breakfast on the day of her departure dressed in a Harris tweed overcoat and skirt, Harris tweed inverted soup-bowl of a hat, lisle stockings and sensible brogues. Given a stout stick, she would have looked like a Victorian lady Alpinist about to climb the Matterhorn. The dogs wandered round her legs, sniffing this unfamiliar figure.

"You look very smart in your uniform," I lied.

"Oh, shut up. You look pretty silly in your clothes, too." She looked down at my dirty, baggy corduroy trousers and her bottom lip trembled.

Vince and Mr. Kilmaster carried the huge trunk and plywood tuck box out to the waiting car.

"I expect it will be lovely when you get there," I ventured when she started chewing one of her plaits and showing some signs of misgiving. "You can have a midnight feast tonight with that chocolate cake Mrs. Dowling's made."

"All ready, darling?" asked our mother, leading the way out of the house with false cheerfulness. "Then off we go."

"Don't forget to look after the ponies," Imogen was not actually crying. And then she was in the car and being driven away.

Mr. Kilmaster took off his old green pork pie hat and waved it at the receding car.

"Well, 'er's gone then," he said, putting his hat on again. "Always was one to leave 'ome hearly, I reckon. Some does, some doesn't. Now don't you fret, Miss Jane, think of all that learnin' 'er'll be getting."

"I'm not fretting."

Bareback, I took him for a long ride through the golden woods

In the saddle-room the pile of rugs in the corner, which was Imogen's reading nest, looked forlorn. I took a halter and went out to the field. It happened to be one of Robin's days for not being caught; each time I got near him he danced away with a wicked gleam in his eye. The lumps of sugar in my palm began to melt. 'Take me,' Imogen's pony Thea seemed to say, standing quietly watching us. Only when I burst into tears did Robin capitulate, giving me a friendly butt in the chest as I put his halter on.

Bareback, I took him for a long ride through the golden woods round by Kicking Horse Pass and Medicine Hat; there were no Red Indian skirmishes that day.

My own 'learnin'' was a source of contention in the family.

"Latin; that's what she needs. A good grounding in Latin. Ero, eras, erat – all that sort of thing. Can't do without it. Any boy of her age would be learning Latin."

"I think she should take up the piano; you're quite musical aren't you, darling?"

"Latin and Greek. Absolutely vital."

"English and French; she can go and have lessons with Armstrongs' Mam'selle."

"They don't talk much English there," I said, remembering the tea party.

"All the better."

"Can I learn geography?" With all these foreigners in the house, Bavarian maids, Swedish governess and old Austrian Mr. Delitz in the barn, I had become quite interested in 'abroad'.

"You can go to a day school in Basingstoke if you like, and learn the whole lot."

"I don't want to go to Basingstoke."

"Bet they don't teach Latin there."

In the end it was decided that I should have Latin, English and algebra lessons with the Vicar of Deane, French with the Armstrongs and piano lessons with two old spinsters who lived near Micheldever Station. All these seats of learning were within galloping distance from home, which suited me very well.

"She can pick up the rest as she goes along," said our father. "She's quite a bright child."

The Reverend Anthony Hardcastle was an elderly, scholarly gentleman who lived very comfortably with his housekeeper in a large, 18th century vicarage: a house unchanged since Jane Austen's time at Steventon. We were to become good friends, and I was to get the grounding in Latin that my father considered so essential. The only problem was staying awake.

An air of post-prandial repose pervaded the house when I let myself in, having stabled Robin, in the early afternoons. A faint aroma left over from the vicar's delicious lunch wafted from the dining room, and in the hall there was the scent of lavender furniture polish and celery. A melodious grandfather clock ticked in the corner by the stairs. In her sitting room, Mrs. Curley, the housekeeper, was fast asleep and very often my tap at his study door startled the vicar from his nap. It would have been better if my lessons had been in the mornings.

"So you have come to 'scramble yourself into a little education', I believe," he said on my first visit, smiling and quoting, unknown to me, from 'Emma'. He was a tall man, stooped now, with a fine head of white hair and the noble Roman profile that one would expect from a Latin scholar.

We sat opposite each other in deep wing chairs on either side of a crackling fire. Leather-bound books lined the walls and the window was hung with red velvet curtains, looped back to let in just a glimmer of Autumn sunshine. I would put my own books on the table between us in the dim light, and we would start to go through my prep before wrestling with the day's translation.

Algebra was the ultimate soporific. Why 'x' should equal 'y' I never did, and never have, understood. The room grew warmer and our eyelids began to droop. As my nights were so restless I had developed the habit of catnapping during the day at an early age. Soon the Reverend Hardcastle and I were fast asleep.

At four o'clock the grandfather clock sang out the hour and Mrs. Curley brought in a tray of tea with delicious tiny sandwiches and cakes. This was the best time, for then the vicar would launch into stories of ancient Rome out of his head not from some dusty book, which I had to translate. He told me of Romulus and Remus, and of the bloodthirsty Emperor Nero and his persecution of the Christians, of Boadicea with her terrifying, slicing, chariot wheels, of the duplicity of Brutus and the assassination of Julius Caesar. In his youth the vicar had been a keen archaeologist and various ancient artefacts, heads with no noses and jugs with broken handles that had lain under the ground for more than two thousand years, stood about on top of the bookcases. Imogen had given me a good introduction to popular English literature, but the excesses of the Greek and Roman Empires were unknown to me; my imagination was fired.

Riding home through the gathering dusk, I was a charioteer charging round the Circus Maximus with the wild applause of the spectators ringing in my ears. Red Indians were temporarily forgotten.

The first time I arrived at the Armstrongs' house in Steventon for a French lesson, I found Miranda and John sitting on the floor in the nursery playing Monopoly.

"Where's Mam'selle?"

"Oh, we've shut her up in her wardrobe for the time being. She's been very annoying lately."

Despite their angelic appearance, these two had an anarchic streak. A muffled thumping came from the French woman's bedroom next door, and you could hear her plaintive cries. "Non, non, non, c'est trop mechant! Ouvres, ouvres mes enfants, je vous en prie!"

This was the reverse of the situation at their cousins, the Lanes, where the Fraulein had the upper hand and did the shutting up herself.

"When will you let her out? I'm supposed to have a French lesson."

"Oh, don't be so boring," Miranda fluttered her dark eyelashes. "Come and play, you can have the top-hat if you like."

The next time I went Mam'selle was at liberty, but as far as the lesson was a concerned she might as well have stayed in the wardrobe. We were soon out of control. You can speak whole sentences in English with your teeth clenched and your lips hardly moving; French, on the other hand, requires constant facial contortions. Miranda and I got 'foux rire' trying to master the Gaelic R, rolling it about in the back of our mouths as though we were gargling. John played the fool, dancing round the table and striking extravagant foreign poses.

"Jibber, Jabber! Jibbairh, Jabbairh, Jabbairh! Oh, Mon Dieu!" he cried. He had the best accent of all.

"Tais toi, John! Be good!" shouted Mam'selle, and then, reading from her book, "Aimez vous les crocodiles?"

This started us off again.

"Non, non, non!"

"Pas du tout!"

"Ooh la la! Par example!"

Miranda and I fell off our chairs, screaming with mock French alarm.

Mam'selle took out a small lace handkerchief and dabbed her eyes. She had become quite nervous since her recent incarceration.

Myself, I preferred Latin. That was a language that you could really get your teeth into.

The Misses Scutt, Daphne and Veronica, were to give me piano lessons to round off my home-based education. They were small, under-nourished old ladies with strong family characteristics rather like the Chichesters: thin faces, beaky noses and long bony hands. They both wore the same sort of clothes, twin sets and tweed skirts that looked homemade, and their grey hair was rolled up over their ears and confined in identical hairnets. Daphne was slightly fatter and had a deeper voice to go with the added avoirdupois.

They still lived in the cottage at Micheldever in which they had been born, and had only left to serve briefly in the F.A.N.Y.'s during the First World War. One imagined that any boyfriends they might have had had been cut down in that terrible massacre; their three passions now were the Church of England, music and cats.

Robin was confined reluctantly in the garden shed and I took my place at the piano. The small front room contained not only the baby grand, but also a harp, a cello, a violin and several music stands, for the Misses Scutt were the musical centre of the neighbourhood. Two of the numerous cats lay on the tiny chintz-covered window seat cleaning their paws.

There was to be no nonsense about scales and arpeggios, and it soon became clear that what the sisters wanted in a pupil, primarily, was an accompanist.

"Bach. Prelude No. 1," declared Veronica, standing beside the piano holding her violin and stabbing the music in front of me with her bow. "Ready? Then off we go."

To my surprise she began to sing loudly with her eyes tight shut and her bowing arm swooping across the strings.

"Arvey Maree-ee-ya, la, lalalalalala la."

I soon got left behind.

"What's the matter?" Veronica's eyes flew open and she glared at me while the violin and bow remained poised in mid air.

"I'm sorry. I'm afraid my sight-reading's not very good."

"So it would seem. Once again, from the beginning..."

"Give the child a chance, Vee," remonstrated Daphne from where she sat in the corner behind the harp, occasionally contributing a rippling chord. "Let her play it through once <u>solo</u> before we have the ensemble. Poor girl, you'll frighten her out of my wits." The cats stopped licking and stared at me with their faraway, impenetrable eyes. Daphne did sometimes get her words muddled up.

"If you insist. Go and put the kettle on then, Daph, while we have a trial run. Ready, Jane?"

It is not a difficult piece and I soon picked it up. By the end of the session I felt myself part of a world-famous trio.

"Now, don't forget to practise," said the sisters when I left. That evening I allowed myself to get carried away as I strummed the prelude on our piano in the hall. My mother came into the room. "Darling, aren't you rather over-doing it? I don't think the pedal was even invented in Bach's day."

Autumn weekends, in true English tradition, were for killing things – mostly foxes and pheasants in our case. One Saturday in late November, when hounds were meeting too far away for Robin and me, I went with my father to a shoot at cousin Benjie's near Overton. I stood behind him in the long valley below Caesar's Belt, a stand of larch planted specially to make the pheasants fly high and fast. At intervals along the ride the other guns waited, dressed more or less like my father, in tweed caps, tweed knickerbockers suits, thick woollen stocking and heavy shoes. Most of them had obedient dogs sitting beside them; in lieu of Sam, my father had me, holding my breath with excitement in the tense silence, straining my ears. The only sound the faint soughing of the wind in the tops of the trees.

Then we heard it, very softly at first like chattering teeth, the tapping of the beaters sticks on the trunks of the trees as they advanced slowly towards us through the wood. My father shifted his feet on the frosty grass where the red November sun had not penetrated and clicked off the safety catch on his gun. I felt the heavy weight of the cartridge bag on my shoulder and the two cartridges held ready between my trembling knuckles. Now the tapping sticks were much louder and closer, and we could hear the blood curdling noises of the beaters as the first pheasants rose rattling out of the trees. All along the valley the guns were blasting off and there was the thumping sound of birds hitting the ground. Two cocks came over us, high and fast as rockets and my father aimed and fired; a right and left, the birds stopped in mid-flight, their heads jerking up and their bodies plummeting down.

"Mark 'em! Mark 'em!" My father broke his gun and I popped the two cartridges in, as we had practised at home. I saw where the pheasants had fallen out of the corner of my eye, as I got more cartridges out of the bag re-loading the smoking gun again and again. For five minutes the valley was turned into a battlefield, with guns blazing, beaters yelling, pheasants streaming overhead and birds falling out of the sky. Then a few last, lone shots and silence, just the acrid smell of the gunpowder drifting in a little blue cloud over our heads. The beaters emerged from between the trees and stood leaning on their sticks and lighting cigarettes as Labradors and Spaniels started picking up the birds and carrying them back to their masters. I had marked the ones my father had shot as best I could, and now began to retrieve them like the obedient dog that he lacked.

The gun on our left was a visiting American who was wearing a Macintosh hat with flaps down over his ears, although it was not raining.

"Hey!" he shouted at me, walking towards us. "That's my bird!"

I looked at the red and gold breast feathers of the pheasant I was carrying.

"Of course it is," said my father. "I knew it at once."

"Pardon me? You knew it at once?"

"Yes, of course! It's got an American flag stuck up its tail; hand it over, Jane."

The American looked embarrassed. "Oh well… I guess…" he began and without finishing his sentence, turned and walked away.

It was the last drive of the morning, and we joined the others walking down from Caesar's Belt to the house for lunch. My father squeezed the back of my neck as we walked along, his gun lying easily over the crook of his other arm.

"Well done, darling; you'll make a first class loader one of these days."

"I did drop some."

"You did very well."

"Was there really a flag in that pheasant's bottom? I didn't see it."

"No, and it wasn't Mr. Weiskipf's bird either."

One of my father's sisters had married into cousin Benjie's family, so our relationship to him was extremely remote. He was an eccentric millionaire with a mean streak; to save money he always insisted on mending his shoes himself, keeping a cobbler's bench, last and awl in a downstairs passage of his large house. A son who fell out of favour was reduced to living in penury in an unfurnished flat in London. Where shooting lunches were concerned, however, he was the soul of generosity, and a large spread was laid on for the guns in the dining room, while the keepers, loaders and beaters feasted in the servants' hall.

All my contemporaries were away at school and I was the only child at lunch that November. I sat beside my father and watched as people helped themselves to the huge steak and kidney puddings in their damask-napkin wrapped basins at the sideboard; Dundee cakes and Stiltons, bowls of fruit and shafts of celery were already on the table. Someone filled my plate and I sat with a Labrador's head on each knee, listening as my uncles and cousins, and their friends discussed the morning's sport. My father was a very good shot and I felt proud when people congratulated him on the very high right and left that he had got at the beginning of the last drive.

"Actually, I think it was my loader that did it," he said. "She just looked up and hypnotised them with those blue eyes of hers."

For a moment I was the centre of attention at our end of the table, and I felt myself turning pink. One of the Labradors took advantage of my distraction and snatched a piece of meat off my fork. There was a shout of laughter and the dog's owner smacked it on the muzzle and sent it off into a corner of the room.

There was Guinness and Beer with the meat and port with the Stilton. The weather-beaten faces round me grew more weather-beaten and the voices louder. I began to wish I was out of doors again.

"I certainly hope those birds of yours will be nice and low and steady this afternoon, Benjie old boy," said Mr. Weiskopf, whose hair stood up in a sort of shorn door-mat now that he had taken off his cap.

Cousin Benjie was lighting a cigar. "Not on your life," he puffed at it, turning it round to inspect its glowing end. "They should be even higher and faster than this morning. Where we're going they really get the wind under their tails. I wouldn't have that third glass of port if I were you."

"Speaking of blue eyes," said Uncle Joe, who was sitting on my other side. "How is that lovely Swedish governess of yours? My word, what a smasher."

"She's gone. She's getting married," I told him coldly. I remembered that funny business in the summer when Aunt Emily had lost him and Mummy had made Karin cry.

"Oh no! What a rotten shame."

After lunch I found my two old friends, Howell and Juffs, the water-keepers, standing in the stable yard with the other beaters. "You come along with us and we'll have some fun. Still got that ole catapult?"

I pulled it out of the back pocket of my trousers. I had had to buy new thongs for it in Winchester, but otherwise it was as good as new.

The local policeman PC Chance, in his Saturday clothes, came over and looked at it. He demanded with mock severity. "What's this then? An offensive weapon?"

"Well it would be if I were a better shot," I replied.

My father suggested that I join the beaters. "But will you manage to load it all by yourself?"

"I'll manage," he smiled, pulling on his cap outside the house. "And you'll be warmer running about with those two old ruffians than you will if you come with me."

There was certainly a nip in the air as we trudged up the long track towards the big beech wood that clothed the side of the hill above the house. The guns would be ranged along the plough on the further side. Ten of the beaters were boys from the local Borstal Institution, clad in blue Burberrys. They looked harmless enough, but it seemed foolish to me to arm them with hefty sticks. I stuck close to Howell and Juffs in case they decided to return to their evil ways.

The men spread out along the brambly edge of the wood and waited for the keeper's whistle: the signal for them to plunge in. A rabbit poked its head out and retreated hastily when it saw Juffs and me standing there; jays shrieked their warning from inside the wood. Otherwise all was still.

Juffs took a flask out of the knapsack on his back and quietly unscrewed it. "Just a little nip to keep the cold out," he whispered, and took a long swallow. I heard the liquid gurgle in his throat as I stood beside him, gripping the stout hazel that I had been given at the house. My heart was beating in loud, steady thumps; what if the pheasants heard it and all flew out the wrong way before the guns were ready?

Faintly the keeper's whistle reached us, and then we were through the brambles and into the edge of the wood, whacking everything in sight with our sticks. Most of the brambles were taller than my gumboots and snatched at my corduroy trousers as I waded through them.

"Yolly yolly yolly brrrr!" yelled Howell, his voice sounding like a football rattle.

"Get up and get out, yer silly beggers!" shouted Juffs.

"Yolly yolly brr!" I echoed, hitting a beech tree with my stick. A grey squirrel ran half way up the trunk and looked down at me, more offended than afraid.

We came to a clearing where a pheasant feeder stood: two straw bales with a sheet of corrugated iron stretched across them. It seemed sad to me that just a few weeks ago the birds had come here for food, trusting in the keeper as their friend, and now at his command we were beating the living daylights out of their cover to make them get up in the air, fly over the guns and be shot. There was no time for remorse, though, as the rattling and tapping and crashing of boots through the undergrowth reached a crescendo round me, and the first pheasants began to take off through the trees. One of them rose vertically from under our feet and a few seconds later there was a loud bang. We were nearer the guns than I had thought.

"I seen that ol' blighter sneaking off from Caesar's Belt this mornin'," Juffs grinned.

"He's sure got his come-uppance now!"

"High high high high high!" yelled Howell, as he battered his way through the wood, level with us.

"Hold the line, lads!" called the keepers when some of the blue-coated Borstal boys to our right plunged forward with too much enthusiasm. There was a positive barrage of gunfire from the plough, as more long-tailed birds sailed out of their cover. I tripped over a root and fell headlong.

"Watch out, Miss Jane, or they'll be taking you for a rabbit!" said Juffs, catching hold of my jacket collar and setting, me on my feet again.

"Are they shooting rabbits as well?" I asked, breathless from my fall.

"Maybe the odd 'un if he looks tasty enough. Yolly yolly yolly brrrrr!"

Then there was space and light and no more trees, and we were out of the wood. A few stray shots and the barrage was over. We stood leaning on our sticks, panting, watching the dogs scurrying backwards and forwards retrieving the dead game and chasing the runners. Juffs took another long swig from his flask and handed it to Howell.

"There," he wiped his mouth with the back of his hand and asked me, "That set your blood a tingling, didn't it?"

"Yes it did."

The farm cart with the patient horse standing at the corner of the wood was beginning to fill up with the brilliant coloured bodies of the dead pheasants, their long tails drooping. It had been a record bag for that drive. Walking towards the cart with the two water-keepers, I saw a dead hare lying in the bottom of a furrow.

"You pick 'im up, but 'old 'im careful," said Juffs. "Them fellers is up to all sorts of tricks."

Gingerly I bent down and grasped the two furry hind legs. It was quite heavy and as I lifted it, a sudden jet of warm liquid shot all over me, drenching the front of my clothes.

"Yargh!" Hastily I dropped the hare and stood staring down at it. The two men laughed until they had to wipe their eyes, and others came over to see what was so funny.

"Is it still alive?" I asked, horrified, feeling warm dampness streaming down my legs and turning cold.

"Alive? 'E'm deader than a doornail, but 'e still got you, didn't 'un! I told you to 'old 'im careful."

"Laugh! You should have seen your face!"

My father came up and tossed a brace of pheasants into the cart. "Enjoy yourself, darling? What's all that stuff on your trousers? Did you fall in a puddle?"

"Oh, Daddy, that hare went to the loo all over me. How did it, if it was dead?"

"What a dirty trick!" My father laughed with the others. "The hare's revenge, eh, Juffs?"

"That's right, sir. Spot on target."

Driving home through the quiet lanes, with mist on the fields and a touch of frost in the air, I felt warm and sleepy, if a bit smelly from the hare's revenge. My father began to sing softly, tapping out the time on the steering wheel.

"Oh Jerry,
That was naughty very,
At a fox you never ought to shoot.
I don't care what people say,
I'll shoot partridges in May!
For I'm Mr. Jeremiah, Esquire...' "

It was already dark when we turned into the drive and the lights of the house lay in yellow rectangles on the gravel. I carried the brace of pheasants that we had been given through to the game larder, their necks silky in my fingers, their long tails trailing behind. Their eyes were tight shut under their blue lids, as though they were deep in thought. The dogs followed me in, jumping at the dangling bodies when I hung them on the hook. I picked Fred up and had my face washed by his pink tongue.

"Phew," my mother pulled a face. "Do go and change, darling; you smell awful." I told her about the hare.

Later, we had tea in front of the fire, and I ate two crumpets dripping with butter and Gentleman's Relish while my father stood by the fireplace stirring his tea so wildly that it slopped into the saucer, as he recounted the day's adventures to my mother.

My head was still full of the great drive at Caesar's Belt and the sight of those hundreds of birds zooming over the trees like cannon balls. It had been a 'cock's only' day, and I wondered about all the hen pheasants left behind in the woods going up to roost in the trees without their men.

Chapter Ten

Our parents were not unmusical. When they were first married, Myra had had some piano lessons with Billy Mayerl in London, and using his technique could swing into tunes from Ivor Novello, Cole Porter and Noel Coward; her rendering of 'Some Day I'll Find You, Moonlight Behind You' brought tears to the eyes. Marcus had only one piece, and would thump out 'In The Mood' with dash and verve when people came to stay. He was also very fond of Mendelsohn's Violin Concerto, which he played a lot on the Radiogram. The old record had a deep scratch across the middle in which the needle would stick; with an oath or two he would get out of his chair and give the massive machine a kick in the guts to send Yehudi Menuhin on his way.

However, they did not seem to appreciate my sessions at the piano, practising for the Misses Scutt, and when I began to emulate the old ladies and accompany myself in an adaptation of 'Oh, For the Wings, For The Wings Of A Dove', they started to spend more and more time in London.

At least, I thought that was the reason. They had recently acquired a tiny flat in Sloane Street, from which my father could be borne away by the office car every morning, altogether more convenient than the tedious train journey from Micheldever. In the evenings there were always cocktail parties, dinner parties, visits to the theatre and dancing till dawn in night-clubs like the Kitcat and the Embassy, for the winter of 1938 seemed to be a frantic time of gaiety for grown-ups.

Life in the country was much more peaceful, and left to my own devices I was having a wonderful time. There was a vague kind of supervision from Mrs. Dowling and the maids, but they did not bother to see that I went to bed on time, or brushed my teeth and hair and washed my hands, the sort of irritating routine that children are usually subjected to. I took my meals as and when I wanted them - in the saddle room reading a book, with

Vince in the woodshed, or up the sycamore tree with my imaginary shipmates. I did not shirk my lessons with the Reverend Hardcastle, the Misses Scutt and the Armstrong's Mam'selle, however, and I cleaned myself up a bit of my own accord for them. I played the piano as loudly as I liked and I started to write a novel with a sea-faring theme and a dash of Oliver Twist, Tom Brown's Schooldays and Midshipman Easy.

The exhausted parents blew in and out for the weekend, sometimes alone, sometimes with friends in tow. "You do look thin, darling," my mother would remark, though she was probably the thinnest person I knew. "Are you eating properly? And when did you last have a bath?"

But they were only rhetorical questions. Our parents had the sort of life-long love affair that binds two people together as though they are one; their children were always of secondary consideration.

In December, Hazel and Doris suddenly died of some kind of terminal guinea pig illness. When I went to feed them in the morning, they were lying in their customary sleeping position, wrapped around each other, but stone cold dead. I rushed to find Vince and tell him of the tragedy.

"Well, blow me down," he said, tilting his cap and scratching the thick hair on the back of his head, as we stood staring at the cage. "They've been and gone and done it now."

"They were all right last night," I sobbed.

"Well, they're all right now, that's for sure; there'll be plenty of them guinea pigs up in Heaven for them to play with. I'll go and get me old spade and dig them a nice big grave."

We wrapped the two small bodies in sacking shrouds and buried them side-by-side under the chestnut tree, behind the stables where the dogs would not find them.

"I still don't see why they had to go and die like that," I sniffed.

"Well, here's no sense grieving," said Vince, lighting a Woodbine. "What's done's done. Tell 'ee what, we'll go and make some proper crosses and carve their names on 'em, shall us?"

"And the date."

"And R.I.P., I reckon," and we left the little mound of newly turned earth and went off to the woodshed to find some proper bits of wood.

After a suitable period of mourning, I was loitering one afternoon at the Railway Cottages, watching Vince skin a rabbit. He sat on an old tree stump near the cabbage patch with the rabbit across his knees and when the smoke cleared, after the latest passage of the London train, I saw him peel the pelt back as though undressing a baby. My father had a rough shoot on the far side of the railway line and I knew that Vince had got the rabbit there where there was a whole housing estate of secret burrows in the banked up earth of the cutting.

"You been ferretin' again, Sir Charles?" I asked.

"Ah. Nothin' like a good ferret. Them's geniuses when it comes to rabbits, them is." He stripped the rabbit's skin off its hindquarters and getting up, laid the naked body on the tree stump and chopped off its head. This he cut in half, exposing the little chamber where its brain nestled.

We put the headless body on the sink by the backdoor. Inside Mrs. Vince dozed as usual in front of the range.

"E'll do nicely with a couple of onions, turnip or two and a bunch of parsley," said Vince, plucking the Woodbine from under his moustache and tossing it into the cabbages. "Now we'll go and give them ferrets their reward."

I followed him round the back of the coal shed holding a halved rabbit's head in each hand, gingerly, by the cold ear, to where the three ferrets writhed and clambered restlessly in their evil-smelling cages.

"You'd better 'ol' the little 'un or 'er'll never get a look in; we'll feed 'er separate." He reached in and pulled out the smallest, and deposited her in my arms when I handed over the 'reward', which the others set upon, tearing the bloody messes to pieces and waving their tails. The little 'un, a pale yellow, looked up at me with hatred in her red eyes and dug her claws into my jersey.

"Ouch!"

Vince put a length of binder twine through her collar and we gave her some of the rabbit's liver to eat on the ground.

"That ole mother o' 'er's is a right bully. She ought to be off on 'er own somewhere. Tell 'ee what," he looked at me thoughtfully for a moment, pulling his moustache. "Why don't you take 'er 'ome with you? You can put 'er in that ole guinea pigs' cage of yours, she'd be right as rain there. Give 'er a real chance in life, that would."

"Would she grow to like me?" I asked, doubtfully.

"Give a ferret plenty to eat and plenty of work and she'll be your best friend. Intelligent! Better than them old guinea pigs, any day."

So that afternoon as the sun sunk rapidly in a yellow winter's sky. I carried my ferret home across the fields in Vince's wooden ferret box with the thick leather strap over my shoulder. I had already named her Fanny. I put clean straw in Hazel and Doris's old hutch and tipped her in. Angrily she clawed the wire and glared at me before starting to explore her new quarters, flashing round the hutch like a small ghost.

Mr. Kilmaster came into the potting shed to put his tools away. "That ole Charlie! Whatever do 'e think you'll be wanting with a ferret, Miss Jane?"

"Catching rabbits, of course. She's very intelligent; she'll be my best friend, quite soon, Mr. Vince says."

"That she will! If she don't eat you first."

At tea at the weekend my mother sniffed. "What's that awful smell? I do hope we haven't got a dead rat under the floor boards again."

I introduced Fanny to Fred in the morning. Fred did his Chinese Emperor act, standing straight-legged and snarling. Fanny ran around sniffing, a yellow wraith, unimpressed by this little black dog who was clearly not a rabbit. I gave them each a raw bantam's egg to eat, which they did nose to nose, and thereafter they did become the best of friends. Next time I went ferreting with Vince, Fred came along, too, and stood guard over the burrows, ready to give chase to anything that might appear. The only time he got cross was when he found Fanny in my bed, which he considered his private territory. My mother got cross, too, so after that Fanny was confined to her cage at night.

On one of my visits to the vicarage at Deane for Latin and algebra, I found the Reverend Hardcastle as usual dozing in front of his fire, but instead of dusty Latin primers, there was a chequered board with antique ivory Chinese chessmen set out on the table in front of him. I studied them while I waited for him to wake up. The Kings and Queens in splendid crowns were severely inscrutable; the knights, on horseback, carried fragile pennons and the castles were like miniature multi-storied dovecotes.

I was afraid that when the vicar woke up the beautiful armies would be put away, but this was not to be.

"The time has come, my dear," he said, when he awoke, "to broaden your mind. I presume that you do not already play chess?"

"No. At home it's either back-gammon or racing demon."

"Very well. Then we shall start at the beginning. A clean slate is so much better than one with a few half-forgotten assumptions scribbled in the corners."

"And we sometimes play animal snap. Imogen's quicker than I am."

"A childish game. Chess is a grown-up game, but you are never too young to start. In China there are already ten year old Grand Masters."

I cupped my chin in my hands and stared at the beautiful little chessmen.

"As you can see, the two sides are ranged against each other like armies ready for battle, and that is right for chess is not really a game – it is war. Strangely enough the King, with his restricted movement, is the weakest piece on the board, and he must be defended at all costs."

"And the Queen?"

"She is a monster. She can do anything she likes. But at the beginning it is wise to keep her in her place, out of harm's way, where she can watch and see how the battle progresses."

I found the Reverend Hardcastle as usual dozing in front of his fire,

The fire crackled in the grate and while the hazy winter sun died outside the window we began to play. When the grandfather clock struck four in the hall and Mrs. Curley brought in the tea, we were engrossed in our fourth game. My head was spinning with the effort of remembering the various movements of my troops, how the knights could hop sideways and the bishops slice diagonally through the field. My heart thumped and my cheeks burned as I planned what seemed a certain checkmate, only to have my marauding piece scooped up by the Vicar and my own King in jeopardy. "Protect, my dear! Protect! Never leave a piece un-guarded."

"Goodness gracious me," said Mrs. Curley, putting the laden tray down on the table by the window. "What sort of a Latin lesson is this, then?"

My parents were also sceptical when I told them at the weekend that the Vicar was teaching me how to play chess.

"It's to broaden my mind," I said complacently. "I can feel it getting broader all the time."

"You are supposed to be learning Latin, English and algebra for your School Certificate, darling, you'll fail it if you don't study properly."

"Oh, don't worry. I'm not much good at algebra, but I wrote an essay about the Roman soldiers guarding Hadrian's Wall in the freezing winter weather with their knees all chapped, because they wore such silly clothes, and Rev. Hardcastle said it was first class. He said it hit two birds with one stone, though I don't know what he meant, really."

My parents looked at each other. "How much are we paying for this mind-broadening experience?" asked my father.

"I can't remember, darling. Goodness, look at the time. You know the Lanes always eat early," and they went off to get dressed for dinner.

Chapter Eleven

Snow fell in December, powdering the thatch on the barn and muffling the fields and woods. Car wheels on the drive made a creaking sound while our footsteps were silent. In the mornings, after roosting in the Macrocarpa hedge all night, the bantams had ice on their trousers and white hats of snow on their topknots. The lawns were criss-crossed with secret footprints of hares, foxes and the spidery traces of birds. The dogs flung themselves about in wild ecstatic games, floundering in the drifts, turning them into whirls of whipped cream. Fred, fully grown now and measuring six inches from paw to shoulder, frequently disappeared, and when rescued carried tinkling balls of ice about on his feathers. His long pink tongue was busy kissing everybody.

Imogen came home for the Christmas holidays, taller and broader than I remembered, and with a chilblain on the end of her nose. We were strangers. "Is it cold at your school," I asked politely.

"Not particularly. I've just got this chilblain, that's all." Her hair was still long, but pulled back into one plait instead of two. She had developed a kind of rolling walk that caused her to collide with doorways and bits of furniture. And she frequently dropped things, like trays of china, when going from room to room.

The parents did not disguise their irritation at her adolescent clumsiness. "For heaven's sake, look where you're going! And don't poke your head." They couldn't leave her alone for a moment. "Don't stand about like that, tuck your bottom in!"

Our mother made her walk about with telephone books on her head to improve her posture. Any self-confidence she still had evaporated with their bullying. Her old caustic wit, however, was still there for me.

"Rev. Hardcastle is teaching me to play chess," I confided when she had changed from her bursting-at-the-seams Harris Tweed uniform back into her old corduroys, and we were standing in the snow feeding the ponies.

"Bernard Shaw says that chess is an excuse for really stupid people to feel intelligent," retorted my sister.

"And I'm learning 'The Gollywog's Cake-walk' on the piano."

"I wondered what the horrible noise was that you were making the other morning. Debussy wrote that for his little daughter; she was about seven at the time."

"She must have been a genius. I'm finding it quite difficult."

"That's obvious. Your education sounds pretty silly to me."

Imogen's beautiful Shetland sheepdog, Brora, was the only person who was really pleased by her return. He lay in the snow watching her with adoring eyes.

After Christmas, the parents arranged for her to go away again, this time to friends of theirs in Gloucestershire. They had a son of fifteen, and lived in the Beaufort country with a stable full of classy hunters. The mother was a well-known bully who mercilessly fagged any young girl who came to stay, making them, among other things, clean the tack, the boots and the hunters.

It was difficult to know whether Imogen wanted to go or not. Half of her personality seemed to have been crushed by a term at Boarding School, confirming me in my belief that the system was a gross mistake. She may have despised my rather haphazard schooling, but I did not want any part of hers.

She came back from Gloucestershire just before the end of the holidays, and that was when we finally got back onto our old familiar footing. We had often risen very early on winter mornings, while the stars were still bright in the sky; we would steal down to the kitchen through the sleepy household, and make ourselves delectable sandwiches of white bread, lots of butter and Demerara sugar. Then out of the back door with the dogs and up to the stables, through the creaking iron gate and past the huge dark form of the barn, where one of Mr. Delitz's orphan owls, grown-up now, would hoot its lonely cry from the rafters.

Before her return I was used to following this routine by myself, and, on one of Imogen's last mornings, I was pulling on my clothes when she popped into my room, fully dressed. "Come one," she whispered, and everything was the same again between us.

It was a magical time of day: the morning star hung low on the horizon while the sky turned from black to velvety purple, and frosty grass crackled under our feet as we ran across the lawn. In the saddle-room we lit the candle in the lantern hanging on its peg, and curled up together on the pile of rugs to eat our crunchy sandwiches. Shadows of our saddles on their iron racks, which Imogen painted red the previous summer, flickered on the wooden walls. A couple of bantam cocks crowed at each other in their squeaky voices from the depths of their evergreen hedge. Through the open top of the saddle-room door we could see the sky changing rapidly from deep lilac to pale duck-egg blue.

"You're quite lucky being here all the time, I suppose," admitted Imogen.

"I think so. Are you dreading going back?"

"It's just the actual going. I'm all right when I get there."

"That's what grown-ups say." I gave Fred a bit of my sugar sandwich and the grains of Demerara clung to his whiskers, making us laugh.

"Sometimes, I dream about sugar sandwiches at school; the food is really ghastly. Someone said you can taste the birds in the custard."

"Well, you've always wanted to go, since you were quite small."

"I know. And I've told you, I don't really mind it when I'm there. It's just that you get to be a bit schizophrenic, living in two different worlds."

"What ever's 'schizophrenic'?"

"Oh, never mind. Let's go and feed the ponies."

I blew out the lantern, my breath smoky in the frosty air. I hoped Imogen would turn back into her original self a bit sooner when the Easter holidays came round; it seemed a pity to have to wait till the very end.

117

A few evenings later we trudged across the fields.

Two days later, off she went again encased in Harris Tweed and shod with sensible shoes. I missed her for a while, but soon had plenty of other things to think about. There was the resumption of my own sporadic education, but more importantly there was my father's decision to up-grade my firepower from the catapult to the 4.10. "You'll never hit a rabbit with that catapult, darling. Now you've got the ferret you'd better have something more serious to pot them with."

I was very excited. We pinned a target on one of the barn doors and I loosed off, managing to hit it once or twice, and already imagining myself the brave Sheriff who saves the Wild West town from the band of marauding outlaws. The feral cats that lived in the barn scooted out between our legs and the dogs gave chase.

My father inspected the target. "Well done, darling, not too bad for a beginner." We ignored the shot that ended up in the thatch. "Keep practising. We'll make you into a crack shot yet."

A few evenings later we trudged across the fields in the hazy dusk to the larch woods, both of us armed to the teeth. We stood in a mossy clearing and waited, straining our ears for the thin high whistling sound of pigeons coming in to roost. Around us the woods were settling down for the night; all we heard was the creak and groan of a broken branch swaying in the wind, the throaty rattle of a pheasant hoisting itself up into a tree, and the scuffling noise of little animals in the dead leaves at our feet.

"Don't move your eyes," my father whispered. "A pigeon can spot the whites of your eye-balls at a hundred yards." I frowned obediently down at my beautiful gun, which my woollen-gloved hands were holding at the ready.

"Here they come," and then I heard it, the faint 'pheeoo, pheeoo, pheeoo' as the first pigeons floated down out of the sky.

We fired almost simultaneously, my father's double-barrelled cracks and my small pop startling the whole wood, sending any pigeons that had come in earlier clattering away over the tops of the trees to find a safer billet.

119

Two dead bodies lay at the edge of the clearing.

"Well done, darling, your first pigeon, good shooting!"

I couldn't believe it. "You don't mean I actually shot one?" I leaned the 4.10 carefully against a tree and went and picked up the two warm limp bodies. "Gosh, can I go and tell Mummy?"

My father was lighting a cigarette, blowing smoke into the frosty air. "Of course, you run on home. I'll hang on here for a while and see if any of them come back. Off you go, Dead Eye Dick!"

I flew on winged feet over the sloping fields, back to the house, a gun in one hand and my pigeon by the neck in the other.

"Mummy! Mummy! I shot a pigeon!"

My mother was impressed. After we had eaten the bird, she had its picked-clean wishbone mounted in a little velvet frame, which stood on the mantle-piece in my bedroom for many years.

It was a long time before my father admitted that both birds were actually his; heaven only knows where my shot went.

In the large wood a flock of pigeons sat in the tops of trees staring down at me, their eye-balls as big as poached eggs revolving in the moonlight.

"Take one child, Taffy," cooed the leader.

"Take two, take two," echoed the others.

"Take two children," agreed the leader, swooping down to a lower branch. "Take two children, Taffy. Take one dog."

I parted the feathery branches of the large tree nearest me, trying to hide from the white eye-balls of the leader. I could see a thread of blood dripping from its beak.

"Take one dog," echoed the other pigeons, their wing feathers whistling as they, too, settled lower down, surrounding me.

"Take Fred, take Fred," cooed the leader in its mild, but menacing voice.

I flung my arms round the trunk of the tree. "No!" I screamed.

"Don't take Fred!"

"Haroo, haroo," cooed the pigeons, all around me now, cutting off my escape. "Take two, take two."

I woke to find myself cold and stiff, in the broom cupboard under the back stairs. There was no Karin now to find me and take me back to bed.

One winter's night, as I sat with my parents by the fire in the hall, the only chimney in the house that did not smoke, there was a thunderous knock at the front door that made us all jump and set the dogs barking.

I was in my pyjamas and dressing gown ready to go to bed, but I opened the door to find the farmer, Mr. Ranger, and his three sons, Harold and Arthur and Donald, standing like pillars of fire in the porch, their breath smoking round their heads in the cold night air. They pushed past me.

"Hello, Ranger! What can I do for you?" asked my father urbanely, standing in front of the fire in his green smoking jacket.

The farmers stood in a row, shuffling their thick boots. Dinah, the young Labrador, put her paws up on the farmer's stomach and tired to push him over. After their dramatic entrance, they seemed at a loss as to the next move.

Mr. Ranger took off his cap, flapped it at Dinah and put it on again. "It's about them 'uns. It's about them 'unnish maids of yours; I want you to whip 'em off."

"Hansi and Bertha?" asked my mother from the depths of her velvet chair. "Why, whatever have they done?"

"They won't leave my boys alone, that's what. Bloody Germans! They're spying for that 'itler, if you ask me."

"What awful rubbish," said my father sternly. "They are extremely anti-Hitler as a matter of fact. They come from good Bavarian families that will probably suffer the most from that regime."

My mother was shocked. "We've had them for nearly two years!"

"I knows you 'ave. For nearly two years they've been buzzin' round my boys like bees round a honey-pot."

Harold, the tallest and best looking honey-pot pushed the hair out of his eyes and grinned sheepishly.

"Well, I'm sure they're good looking fellows," said my father, at which Donald, the youngest one who dribbled, tucked his head into his shoulder with embarrassment, "and from what I've seen, there's been a little bit of encouragement coming from your camp."

He stared hard at Harold, and walked across the room to the drinks tray. "Now, what'll you have? Whisky? It's terrible weather for turning out in the middle of the night and making wild aspersions."

"Now don't you try softening us up with 'ard liquor. We're here on business. There's penalties for them that's 'arbouring spies. Down, dog, down."

I got hold of Dinah by her collar and we went and sat under the piano.

"Oh, come on, Dad," said Harold, who had been eyeing the whisky decanter. "We're all friends here. I'm sure Mr. Chichester's done nothing wrong."

"I'll speak to the girls in the morning," conceded my mother and soon they were all having jolly drinks, although she did not invite them to sit down.

Half an hour later, after a lively discussion about the lambing season and what crop they were going to plant in which field during the coming year, the farmer and his sons left, quite a lot pinker in the face. My father, I had heard some of the weekend visitors say, could charm the birds off the trees.

My mother did talk to Hansi and Bertha in the morning and there were tears all round, for far from spying for Hitler or having designs on the Ranger boys, they admitted that they had decided to go back to Germany.

"Are you sure this is wise? The situation is very difficult over there at the moment," my mother counselled.

"Everything is terrible in Germany, Madame, but we must go back to our families," cried Bertha.

"It is decided, we must go back. We have been happy here, but we must go back," sobbed Hansi. My mother lent them her handkerchief as their blue eyes over-flowed. It was a sad moment and we were to miss Bertha's yodelling as she did the washing up, and Hansi trilling 'The Blue Danube' while she twirled a feather duster. We never heard from them again.

After they left, Mrs. Kilmaster came across the field every morning to help in the house. She was certainly not a spy. Her favourite tune was 'Land Of Hope And Glory', which she whistled through a missing front tooth as she waddled from room to room in a cloud of dust of her own making, wearing a hair-net over her corrugated hair and a floral apron. Most of the morning was taken up with long cosy chats with Mrs. Dowling and her husband over the big brown teapot at the kitchen table.

Chapter Twelve

There were very few visitors during the winter months; our draughty old house with its own (unreliable) electricity generator and eccentric water pump was known as one of the coldest in England. But in the spring the weekend house parties started up again, though now a lot of the men who came were wearing uniform.

A stretch of farmland near Micheldever had been turned into a military transit camp and some of the parents' friends were stationed there. They would come to us for good food and, they hoped, a hot bath. I did not realise that world war was imminent, however, until I rode into the Armstrong's yard one day for my French lesson to find two men hoisting a lorry load of sacks of rice into the hayloft. I knew that the Armstrongs were inclined to give their ponies unsuitable food, like Marmite sandwiches and chocolate biscuits, but this was ridiculous.

"It's the war," explained Miranda and John. "Mummy remembers the last one. They had no rice pudding for four years. She's determined not to be caught like that again."

No rice pudding for four years sounded like heaven to me. "Won't the rats eat it?"

"With any luck," said John. "Why is your pony so hairy?"

"It's his winter coat, it hasn't all come out yet." Robin's winter coat was about four inches long.

"Ours has. But then ours wear New Zealand rugs in the winter."

"How sissy." I put Robin in one of the stables and glanced upwards at the loft full of rice. "What will it be like, d'you think, if there's a war?"

"Great," enthused John. "I'll probably join up. Bang! bang! Aargh! Bang bang!" He ran around in circles acting both sides at once, his fair hair flopping about.

"Do they take boys of six in the Army?"

"I'm very big for my age." He drew himself up to his full height. He was. Both he and Miranda were twice my size. "Let's play soldiers, Jane can be the enemy."

"Must I?"

"I'll be the Red Cross," said Miranda.

The summerhouse under the tall beech trees at the top of the lawn became the enemy camp.

"Anh anh anh anh anh," rattled my machine gun out of the window. A steam of bullets hit John as he tried to storm the wooden steps. He kept on coming.

"You're dead!" I shouted. "I should have had my 4.10 with me."

"Only wounded," John clutched his side and staggered into the hut.

I raked him again with withering fire. "There. Now you're completely dead."

"I'm not! You missed!" We wrestled on the floor and I hit my head quite hard on a folded deck chair.

Miranda appeared in the doorway with a white handkerchief tied round her forehead. "Right, you're both badly wounded. This is the hospital. I'll do my best to save you, but you'll probably die in the end."

Obediently John and I lay side by side on the floor, while Miranda took our temperatures and bandaged our wounds.

"This is boring," said John after a while, sitting up. "I'm really the Doctor. Let's cut off Jane's legs."

"There's nothing wrong with my legs! It's my head that hurts."

"No dear, it's your legs," said Miranda gravely. "Hold her down, Doctor, while I pull off her trousers."

"Very well, Nurse."

"Help!" I screamed into John's grey flannel shorts as he sat on my chest. I thrashed about, wriggling and struggling. I could feel the scratchy wooden floor under my behind and a cold draught where my trousers and knickers should have been. "Get off!"

"I'm afraid this poor soldier's delirious. Shall I give him an injection,

Doctor, for the pain?"

"By all means, Nurse. In his bottom."

"No! No!" With a heave I sent John flying just as the dulcet tones of Mam'selle called across the garden.

"Coo-ee! Où êtes vous? Venez, venez vite! Au travail, mes enfants."

"Coming," shouted Miranda. "Drat the woman, that was fun."

"Not for me," I grumbled, red in the face, pulling on my knickers.

"You're just a bad sport." Miranda set off towards the house.

Later, hostilities ceased as we sat at Mrs. Armstrong's feet on the pale pink carpet in the drawing room. In her soothing voice she read us a chapter from 'The Jungle Book'. We were really too old for this ritual and after a while Miranda and John wriggled themselves behind her chair and began to play Jacks. Noticing nothing, their mother read on; I got the feeling that if war did break out, if a bomb fell or a regiment of German soldiers burst into the room, Mrs. Armstrong would just carry on reading. I watched her, fascinated, and in my mind I composed the next chapter of my own novel.

There was no reason why my hero, Thomas, should not have a spell in the jungle. I could see him in his loin cloth, standing on the Council Rock in the moonlight hurling the fire-pot to the ground in front of the cowering animals, though the transition from white flannelled hero of the first eleven, as he was in Chapter Two, might be a bit difficult to bring about.

"There, that's all for tonight, darlings," said Mrs. Armstrong, shutting the book with a snap. "Darlings?" John and Miranda wriggled into view. "Oh, there you are. Jane dear, I do believe you were half asleep. It's time you went home, you know, or would you like to stay the night? It's beginning to get dark."

"No thank you, Robin and I can find our way in the dark."

"I think Mowgli's silly," said Miranda. "It would have been better if the tiger had eaten him in the beginning."

"Then there would have been no story," said Mrs. Armstrong.

"It's a boys' book." John climbed over the back of the sofa "You can't understand it because you're only a girl."

"There's nothing wrong with being a girl," countered Miranda, although I didn't agree.

"Anyway, why doesn't he wear any clothes? A girl would have found some clothes and worn them."

"Some girls don't wear any clothes." John slid off the sofa on to the floor. "Jane took off her clothes in the summer house this afternoon."

"I didn't!"

Mrs. Armstrong raised her arched eyebrows and looked at me.

"You did!"

"*You* did."

Mrs. Armstrong sighed and picked up her tapestry. "Run along now, darlings, time for bed."

"I bet Mowgli didn't go to bed as early as this," grumbled John as we went back upstairs. "I bet he had more fun than we do playing about with all those wolves," and he gave an imitation of the Stranger's Hunting Call, and slid down the banisters to the bottom again.

"I saw a wolf in the zoo once, and he smelled awful," said Miranda.

"Worse than Jane's knickers?" asked John, rejoining us.

We had a final tussle on the landing and then I went out to the stables to saddle Robin. I was glad I was a free agent, riding away through the misty fields and woods while the Armstrongs knelt at their nursery sofa saying their prayers, their hearts full of new ideas for torturing visitors. It had given me a funny feeling in the pit of my stomach when they undressed me in the hut, half beastly and half exciting, which I could not quite understand. It had been a strange afternoon; I certainly hadn't learnt much French.

My Latin, however, was making great strides, we were already into Tacitus and his accounts of Agricola's subjugation of the British. But one day I found that Rev. Hardcastle was, also, preparing for war. Instead of the usual pile of books, there was a green baize cloth spread over our worktable and he was absorbed in polishing the eagle on top of a huge Prussian helmet. Beside it lay a vicious looking sword in a delicately embossed scabbard. *"Bello praeparationem facio,"* he said, smiling up at me.

"So I see," I sat down and stared at my face in the gleaming metal of the helmet. "But if you wear this helmet, Rev. Hardcastle, people will think you are the enemy."

"They will soon be disillusioned. We will cut off the German's heads with my grandfather's sword, when you have cleaned it up." He passed me the Brasso. I drew the long sword out of its scabbard. The sharp tip was stained with rust.

"Gladio sanguineus est," I ventured.

"Bravo! And you may be right. But I believe the old fellow was given the ignominious task of slicing sugar-beet for cattle in peace-time; that stain might be the residue."

"We will destroy the enemy like Boadicea and the Iceni!" I enthused as the dull blade began to gleam under my rubbing.

"Up to a point. Boadicea was an undisciplined woman by all accounts with a terrible lust for bloodshed as you remember; she poisoned herself in the end. If the present difficult situation really comes to war and the Germans invade, we shall do better than that. It's no good hacking people to pieces and then doing yourself in as soon as you get repulsed."

We polished in silence for a while. I imagined the Vicar mounted on a grey charger wearing the splendid helmet and defending the village of Deane with his trusty sword from the plundering hordes, looking a little like Don Quixote. I would be his Sancho Panza riding Robin at his side, backing him up.

"But now, we must not neglect your education," he cut in, and as if reading my thoughts, "conjugate for me, if you please, the verb *spoliare, to plunder*, while we work."

After tea we played chess and he endeavoured to teach me the Sicilian Defence. Lessons with Rev. Hardcastle were rather like stepping onto a magic carpet, you never knew to where you were going to fly.

Imogen returned for the Easter holidays, bigger and clumsier than ever, and the parents resumed their bullying ways. They were like two terriers worrying a bone and could not leave her alone; her every movement round the house causing a stream of criticism.

"Don't sit on the arm of the chair! Sit in it properly, and with your legs together, if you please."

"Must you run down the stairs like a herd of elephants?"

"See if you can carry the coffee tray out to the pantry without dropping it this time, darling. We have not got an inexhaustible supply of china." And the familiar – "Don't poke your head!"

The head poking was a kind of mania; neither Imogen nor I really knew what they were on about. I suppose, like a boxer, she had taken to leading with her chin to parry their jibes; it seemed to me a normal reaction, if a little ungainly. I felt sorry for her and embarrassed that the parents' attitude towards me had not changed.

My poor sister withdrew more and more to our safe refuge in the saddle room, and the rug pile where she sat reading with her dog Brora for company. He was a soothing and even-tempered dog who got on well with everybody, his only enemies in our sheltered world were cats. Although we had none in the house, and never a cat as a pet, several of them lived on the farm: killing rats, mice and small birds, and bringing up their kittens in secret corners of the stables and the barn. We ignored them and they us, but they loved teasing the dogs and in particular Brora. As he followed Imogen up to the stables or around the garden, they would stand in his path and hiss, waving their tails and arching their backs. Then when he bounded at them, they would dash up the nearest trellis or espaliered fruit tree and make faces at him from above. Some wild chases ended with all the dogs pursuing the cats into the barn. The thwarted animals stood, barking their heads off at the foot of the broad ladder that lead to the hay-loft as the felines flew up it to safety.

None of the dogs had ever ventured up the wooden slats until one terrible day when Brora, goaded beyond reason by a marmalade cat with a long wavy tail, chased her to the top. Once in the hayloft the cat panicked and jumped out of the open gable, landing like thistledown some twenty feet below. Brora, his beautiful silky brown and white coat flying as he leapt, followed.

I heard Imogen's scream as I was coming down from the ponies' field and ran towards the sound. I found my sister on her knees below the hay hoist. On the ground lay Brora, not moving, not trying to get up; every now and then licking the salty tears that poured down Imogen's face as she cradled his head.

He had broken his back. Half an hour passed before the vet came and put him out of his agony.

For the rest of the holidays the parents' attitude towards Imogen softened; they were kinder to her and took her to London for treats. They promised her a puppy, but at the time Imogen said she would never have another dog as long as she lived.

Chapter Thirteen

In May, my ship, the sycamore tree, produced a lot of neatly folded green parcels, which as the weather grew warmer opened into the familiar five pointed leaves. I took the rope ladder out of its winter quarters under my bed, and hung it up. With all the talk of war that I could overhear at the weekend house parties, I decided that the ship should be converted from a wind-jammer into a fast, sleek-lined Destroyer. When he came to spend his leave with us, my cousin Dick who was in the Navy brought me a real sailor's cap from his ship, the Prince of Wales. And this I wore clamped to my head while I supervised the re-fitting.

I had not been near the barn since Brora's tragic accident, making a wide detour down the path between the herbaceous borders, but one day I heard some long-forgotten noises coming from what I always thought of as Mr. Delitz's end of the big building. Looking inside I saw him standing there among his antique collection of belongings.

"Nobody told me! When did you come?" I asked, running into his outstretched arms, feeling his familiar bristly cheek against mine.

"Like the rotten penny, Old Delitz turns up again," he smiled, showing his gold teeth. He pushed his spectacles back up his nose and looked at me. "Well, little Jane – not so little any more. You seem to have grown upwards, if not outwards. Tell me what you have been doing without old Delitz all this time."

Seeing him there with his easel and the old tin bath and the dreadful porridge saucepan, it was as if the clock had been turned back to the carefree days of the previous summer: as if Karin had not got married, Imogen had not gone away to school and changed into a different person, Hansi and Bertha were still here and Hazel and Doris, and Brora had not died. I did not know where to begin telling him about all the changes to my life.

"I've missed you," I began. "Did you have your exhibition?"

He pushed his spectacles up onto his forehead and then pulled them down again. "The world is full of stupid people, my dear Jane. They run around like mice on a tread-mill and have no time to stand and look at beautiful things. No, I did not have my exhibition."

"What a shame. Shall I help you un-pack?"

We wrestled with the big umbrella, the primus-stove, the easel, the saucepans and the extremely vicious camp bed, which had a way of pinching your fingers, however cautiously you treated it. I sat on it, when we had finally beaten it into submission, and looked through one of the portfolios of the old man's drawings. There were several new sketches for portraits of people I did not know jumbled up with landscapes and cows and full-bottomed trees that I recognised from last summer.

"One thing I have been doing," I confided, as I had no one else. "I've started writing a book."

Mr. Delitz came out from behind the screen where he had been setting up the tin bath. "A book!" he cried, as one might say 'a dinosaur!' 'an earthquake!' or some such unusual event. "Is it a thriller?"

"Well, it's quite thrilling in parts."

"Is it about a bandit with curling moustachios who carries pretty ladies away on the back of his horse?"

"Not exactly. It's about a boy called Thomas who has some quite good adventures. At the moment he's in Africa; he's just adopted a lion called Leo."

"Leo! That is a splendid name." I remembered that it was also Mr. Delitz's own. "No book with a lion called Leo in it can possibly be anything but a best-seller."

He began to pump the Primus. He handed me the kettle. "Now if you will go and fill this from the stable tap, the author and the artist will have a cup of tea. And look!" He undid a small parcel that was amongst his painting things and revealed a delicious-looking, very dark chocolate cake. "Fritzi, my wife, has been on holiday in Vienna and she brought me back this Sacher-torte for just such an occasion as this. We shall celebrate my return and drink to a long, hot summer."

As we had our tea sitting amongst the half un-packed bundles, I told him that the maids had gone back to Germany and about the Rangers bursting in with their accusations in the middle of the night.

"They may have been right. Those girls could have been spies. Many German girls have been sent over here to infiltrate English families, find out as much as they can and if possible marry Englishmen so as to go, as we say, under cover. The fact that the farmer rejected Hansi meant that her usefulness here was over, she would not meet anyone else."

I was deeply impressed that we could have had spies in the house and even that the Germans should have thought us worth spying on.

The chocolate cake was wonderful. "Ach so," said Mr. Delitz. "It may be many years before we taste Sacher-torte again."

"That's what the grown-ups keep saying. Is there really going to be a war, do you think?"

"There already is a war going on in Europe, my dear Jane," the old man's bristly grey face creased with sadness. "Fritzi saw terrible things in Austria; the Nazi party is totally unprincipled. It is only a matter of time before Great Britain comes to the rescue, at least, I hope so."

"Don't you worry; we will," I said staunchly.

Fred ambled into the barn to find us, wagging his newly plumed grown-up tail, a picture of peace and stability.

"Ah, here comes the emperor!" Mr. Delitz picked him up and Fred covered his face with wet kisses. "It is a small nose, but a good one!" he pinched the black button and gave Fred some cake. "It is clear that he can smell Sacher-torte a mile away."

It was to be a long hot summer, golden day following golden day, and my tutors decided to make the most of it.

In June, Rev. Hardcastle set off to explore a newly discovered Iron Age settlement in Wales and at the same time the Misses Scutt decided to walk the South Downs Way. It was a daring venture for them and I wondered if they would survive it. They seemed immemorially old to me, though they were probably in their fifties. Mrs. Armstrong took a cottage by the sea in North Cornwall and up-rooted all the children and Mam'selle. They each re-iterated the general theme that this might be the last peaceful summer for some time. I wondered how anyone could think of fighting a war in such glorious weather.

Rev. Hardcastle left me a list of books to read, Mam'selle some French poetry to memorise and the Misses Scutt gave me patriotic pieces of music, such as 'It's A Long Way To Tipperary' and 'Rule Britannia', to practise on the piano. I put them all aside to wait till the days grew cooler.

Free as a bird I began to live like one, either at the top of some tree or lying hidden in the long grass at the edge of a cornfield up by the larch wood watching the birds. A flock of plovers had hatched out their young, in shallow scrapes amongst the slender green blades of spring wheat. The corn afforded little cover and I was fascinated to see how the hens educated the tiny chicks about the dangerous world into which they had been born. They seemed to have an in-built discipline far superior to that of the human race, and reacted instantly to her different calls if a predator, such as a kestrel, hovered overhead - either freezing in the nest or scattering to hide while the mother acted as a decoy.

Sometimes I begged a sandwich from Mrs. Dowling and rode away for a whole day on Robin, now gleaming in his bright bay silky summer coat. About eight miles away, on the other side of Overton, there was an escarpment laced with bridle paths, where you could gallop up to the top and feel like a bird, looking down on the great sweep of land far below. There I would dismount and tie Robin to some bush where he could nibble the grass, while I lay on the ground eating my sandwich, listening to the larks and watching the rabbits scuttling into their burrows.

I dropped into the house for occasional meals, sunburnt and dirty, with grass in my hair.

"Hello, Mowgli," said Imogen when she came home for the summer holidays. "Why don't you get your hair cut? And what are you trying to do with your hands? Win the Black Fingernail Championship of the World?"

Briefly the parents attention was drawn to me. We were having lunch. "Go and wash your hands, darling," said my mother. "And Imogen's quite right, try and comb your hair."

"Must I?" I stuck my tongue out at Imogen as I passed her chair.

"The child's becoming a savage," I heard my father say mildly as I left the room. "No feminine instincts of any kind."

I hovered outside the door on my way to the gents.

"What are you going to do about her?" asked Imogen sternly. She seemed to have become more assertive during her third term away. "Why doesn't she go to school? Has she got any friends of her own age?"

"She's doing quite well with her lessons. As for friends, she seems to prefer animals to her contemporaries. Some children do." I was pleased to hear my mother defend me and continued on my way to wash my hands.

As I scrubbed ineffectually at my nails, I looked at myself in the glass above the basin. I didn't look like Mowgli. My eyes were blue and my face though brown, was not brown enough. I tugged at my long hair with a comb. It was bleached almost white by the sun; his was black. I quite liked the idea though. Next time I climbed a tree I tried swinging hand over hand through the branches. I slipped and fell from quite a high one, and landed in one of Bluebell's cowpats.

Peace descended when Imogen was sent off again, this time to stay with the Gloucestershire people at their summer place in the Isle of Wight. The parents soon forgot about my unkempt appearance, for the weekenders were now in full swing and they had plenty of other things to think about. The tennis players in their short shorts and long flannels, the cocktail drinkers and the backgammon enthusiasts had to be entertained.

At night, they danced till dawn in the hall under my bedroom; Fred and I lay listening to the radiogram, the piano and the laughter. "Tonight, tonight I must forget – music, Maestro, please." Every Saturday night seemed to be like the ball in Brussels on the night before the battle of Waterloo that Rev. Hardcastle had told me about, and in the morning a lot of people were in a bad temper.

In the kitchen Mrs. Dowling was over-stretched. A maid arrived from Jersey, called Jessie, to help out; it was not long before she took up with Harold Ranger where Hansi had left off. As Jersey is part of the United Kingdom, the farmer's family did not object.

The Goodwood house party came and went as usual, and in August the parents were off to Scotland to stay with some cousins who had taken a grouse moor. They would be away for more than a fortnight. On the evening before they left, I lay on the ground beside my mother's chair in the garden. My father came out of the house carrying their drinks. The wings of black hair over his ears were beginning to turn a bluish grey; I supposed it was because of worry over the war, or perhaps just exhaustion from their hectic social summer.

The dogs sprawled panting in the shade that was deepening under the shrubs and trees. My mother put her hand down on my head and stroked my hair; she made few affectionate gestures so when they came, they were all the more valuable. I felt ineffable sadness creeping over me.

"I don't like leaving you here alone for so long, darling. Are you sure you'll be all right?"

"She ought to go and stay with friends of her own age," said my father, putting the tray down on the table and beginning to mix gin and tonics in the tall glasses. "The Leggatts, the Campbells; they'd have her; she's getting to be too much of a loner."

"She doesn't want to," I said, copying his third person mode. "She likes being by herself."

I put my head down on my arms and watched an ant trying to carry a large leaf up the side of a slab of crazy paving. My mother lit one of her flat Turkish cigarettes, and a cloud of midges hanging in mid-air scattered as she exhaled a long blue line of smoke. She persisted, "I wish we could take you with us, but you'd be bored; there'll be nothing but grown-ups."

"Honestly, I'll be fine. I'm here by myself most of the time as it is!"

"Yes, I suppose you are," she sighed. "Anyway, we'll ring up."

"Dammed expensive, ringing up from Scotland," said my father, rattling the ice in his glass.

In the morning, after Mr. Kilmaster had rolled the big green Ford down to the front door and while the business of packing it up with their enormous amount of luggage was in progress, my mother played the piano in the hall. My father never started on a journey or came home from one without a tremendous fuss and she knew from experience that it was better to keep out of the way. Meanwhile the Kilmasters and I helped to cram the suitcases, gun-cases, fishing rods, shooting sticks, cartridge bags, Macintoshes, race-glasses, umbrellas and golf-bags into the car in a way that would still leave room for our parents in the front seats.

My father, in his shirtsleeves, grew increasingly agitated and red in the face. The dogs, knowing they were to be left behind climbed in and tried to make themselves invisible amongst the pile of sporting luggage.

"Get *out*, Pangloss! Come *here*, Sam, you old fool! For goodness sake, Jane, hang onto the dogs. No, Dinah, I'm sorry, you can't come with us. And get that landing net off the gear lever, somebody – how am I supposed to drive?"

It was almost as bad as packing up Mr Delitz; at least they didn't have any saucepans.

At last everything was stacked to his liking. He climbed into the driving seat and began to hoot the horn loudly for my mother. With her shingled hair and in her pale linen suit, she emerged from the house looking cool and unruffled. She carried only her canvas covered crocodile dressing-case with, as I knew, its rows of dear little cut-glass jars and bottles with silver tops engraved with her initials.

"Oh no! Not another case! There's no room for anything more!"

"It's all right, darling; I'll put it under my knees."

Mrs Dowling rushed out of the house with their picnic hamper. My father protested until that, too, went under my mother's long, slim, elegant legs. Through the open door she gave me a hug and a kiss. "Goodbye, darling, be good. Goodbye everybody, goodbye, goodbye!"

"Look after the place, old girl." My father leaned across her to kiss me as well. "You're in charge now."

The big-white-walled tyres turned, churning up the dusty drive and we all waved, Mr. Kilmaster, as usual, flourishing his pork pie hat.

Mrs. Dowling was the first to break the silence, looking at her watch, "Bless me if it isn't time for elevenses. And you come in and have a nice glass of barley water, Miss Jane, this hot weather."

"That's right, it'll do you good," said Mrs. Kilmaster.

"No thank you, I've got things to do."

"I don't know. Proper little tomboy, that one," I heard them muttering among themselves as they went indoors.

"Huh! I'm in charge now, you know, Daddy said so. Get on with your work, slaves!" I pretended to tell them as I slipped away across the empty garden, gathered speed through the dell and finally hoisted myself up the rope ladder into the sycamore tree and my secret world of swaying green leaves and blue sky.

HMS Dalasenus, one of the Navy's newest and most powerful Destroyers, was on ocean-going trials in the Bay of Biscay. The phoney war was at its height and unknown to them an enemy submarine lurked in the murky waters of the bay.

Captain Victor Harrington, RN, was in charge. He stood on the bridge beside the first mate; his cap tipped over one eye and his pipe clenched between his teeth, scanning the wine-dark sea.

At midnight he was preparing to turn in when there was a blinding flash and a huge explosion as a torpedo struck them amidships. Screams were heard below decks.

"We've been hit, sir!" cried the First Mate.

"So it would appear, Number One," said his Captain, with icy calm.

The foredeck tilted at an angle of 45 degrees as the waves crashed over the stricken ship. Bells rang. The bo'sun staggered up from below, streaming with blood. "The engine room's holed, sir, and the radio's out of action!"

"Give the order to abandon ship, Mr. Mate. And don't panic."

"Aye aye, sir!"

Within minutes the crew had manned the lifeboats and were being lowered into the heaving seas. Puffing at his pipe Harrington remained on the bridge. The First Mate lurched back through the wind and rain. The noise of the storm was deafening. Where the torpedo had struck a huge fire was blazing.

"Last boat ready to leave, sir! Are you coming?"

"Carry on, Number One. Set a course for Gibraltar and see if you can get help. I'll stay with the old lady until you return."

"But, sir! We can't leave you here all alone! She might go down at any minute!" As if agreeing, the ship screwed to starboard and sank a little lower into the white-topped waves.

"A Captain's duty is to remain with his ship; avast now, save yourselves while there's still time."

Respectfully, the First Mate saluted his beloved captain who, squaring his broad shoulders, had turned away and set his face towards the Union Jack, still fluttering from the stern.

"That's a brave man, lads," said the First Mate, blinking back the tears as he took the tiller and the life-boat rolled away from the sinking ship. "We'll be lucky if we see his like again."

Mrs. Dowling went off to Bognor for her annual holiday. Mr. Delitz got a commission to draw some neighbour's children; they bore him away in a smart cart one morning.

"I'll be back soon, little Jane!" he said plaintively, clutching his painting gear as he got in. I wondered if they would give him porridge with black current jam for breakfast.

I took to sleeping in my hammock under the sycamore tree,

Jessie, a friendly girl, seemed to spend a lot of time making hay with Harold.

I was in charge. There was plenty to do in the daytime looking after the dogs and bringing in the ponies to the cool stables from their fly-ridden paddock. Mr. Kilmaster taught me how to milk Bluebell, the cow, and I had domino sessions and ferreting excursions with Vince. But at night the house seemed sad and empty. I took to sleeping in my hammock under the sycamore tree, waking in a tent of leaves silvery in the moonlight. Barn owls hooted across the lawns, and the shadows of the house and barn lay behind them like the trains of long black dresses.

One morning coming into the kitchen, after an early ride, to get some breakfast I found Jessie's newspaper lying on the table. The front page showed a large black square with the date written inside it. 'September Third, 1939.' I read, 'Britain declares war on Germany.'

In my den in the barn where I did my writing, I pushed Thomas's adventures to one side and took out my diary. Copying the newspaper I pencilled in a black square round the date.

"So far this has been the happiest year of my life," I wrote. "And now look what happens! The grown-ups have started a war."

My gasmask smelt of hot rubber inside
and I never could see out of it.

PART TWO

Chapter One

My father had been wounded in Palestine during the First World War. A sniper's bullet had whizzed through the Achilles' tendon area of his left foot and lodged in his right. Gangrene set in, which was diagnosed as measles, so he was put in a fever hospital; amputation was seriously considered. Luckily he was sent home to Devon before this drastic step was taken and there liberal doses of clotted cream speeded up the healing process. Although he did not have a noticeable limp in later life, his right foot remained rigid and he was therefore ineligible for active service in the Second World War.

Nevertheless, our parents hurried back from Scotland that first week of September 1939, with the car loaded to the roof as before. Some American friends who had been staying with them at the shooting lodge decided instead to send their luggage on ahead with their servants, and took tickets for them and the luggage on the liner Lusitania. She was to be torpedoed in mid-Atlantic with the loss of many lives.

Ration Books and gas masks were issued. Mrs. Dowling doled out our butter ration in little personalised earthenware pots that were put out on the dining room table. Meanwhile, the camp at Micheldever began to fill up with the parents' Army friends; they started dropping in for breakfast, lunch, tea, dinner and baths. Marcus and Myra were always delighted to see them, but I was not so sure. One such friend used up the whole of my butter ration on a piece of ginger cake. "By Jove, that was good! The Army marches on its stomach, you know!"

My gas mask smelt of hot rubber inside and I never could see out of it. I used it for dealing with Fred when he had a dirty tail.

Vince and I augmented the family's rations with rabbits from the warren beyond the railway line. I was becoming a little more accurate with the 4.10. One day when we were pegging the nets over some of the burrows preparatory to slipping Fanny and Gladys inside (for they were good friends now) he made an extraordinary announcement: "You'd better watch out for that Robin of yours. He'll be getting his call-up papers soon. They'll be needing every horse they can get their hands on before this lot's over."

"But, Sir Charles! Surely they wouldn't take *him!* He's much too small. Besides, Daddy says this war will be fought with tanks and armoured cars and things; he says they'll never use horses again after what happened last time."

I knew that one of my uncles, who was in the Queen's Bays, had lost the whole of his troop of chargers before the end of November in 1914. He had a photograph of them at Aldershot in the summer, all lined up on parade, proud and gleaming: requisitioned hunters, mostly. The cream of Leicestershire, he called them. All to be slaughtered by an enemy not their own, crazed with terror and seldom killed outright. Such a fate was unthinkable for my pony.

"They'll find a use for him," the old man said complacently, tapping the last peg in and straightening up. "As for being small, my ole mule Daisy, who never needed feeding but just a couple of newspapers a day, she taught Jerry a lesson or two. Heaved them guns around like one o'clock, ole Daisy did. Bought it in the end, of course, but if you'd have tried telling her she was too small she'd have given you a bloody good kick, I reckon, 'eroine of the Somme, she were. Right let's get to work. Ferrets in!"

I pulled Fanny out of my shirt and shoved her down the nearest rabbit hole. I was seriously worried and wanted to get back to the house to see if Robin was still there. I no longer cared whether we caught any rabbits or not.

That evening I gave the pony a severe talking to. "If anyone comes for you," I told him, "for instance when I'm not around, there are two things you can do. Either gallop off and hide in Whatnot Wood where they can't find you, or else pretend to be hopping lame, like you do sometimes when you don't want to go for a ride. Understand?"

Chewing a mouthful of grass, Robin stared pensively into the distance. Was he already hearing bugle calls? Vince had said that horses loved wars. I put my arms round his neck and begged him not to join the Army.

In the end, Mr. Kilmaster was the only one of our household to get his call-up papers. "We shall miss you very much," said my mother, formally shaking the unlikely warrior's hand when he came over to the house to say goodbye, with Mrs. Kilmaster, red-eyed, beside him. "But I'm sure you will cover yourself with glory!"

It was an emotional moment and we all stood about awkwardly.

"I'll do my best, 'm. And Miss Jane will be all right looking after Bluebell, 'er's a dab hand at the milking."

"He cares more for that old cow than he does for me," sniffed Mrs. Kilmaster.

"And don't forget to lift the dahlias, 'm."

"We won't. But I expect you'll be home again before the first frost. Don't worry, we'll look after the garden <u>and</u> Mrs. Kilmaster."

"As if he cared!" said his wife with a loud sob, dabbing her eyes with her apron.

"And I've stacked the runner bean poles in the barn for next year, in case that Vince goes and cuts them up for kindling. And the Christmas bulbs are all on the bottom shelf in the apple room where it's nice and dark."

It was a very long drawn-out farewell, as every time the gardener seemed about to take his leave he thought of some more instructions for us. At last, muttering disconsolately that he didn't know how we were going to manage without him, he went. Later we heard that he had been sent from the Winchester depot, inexplicably, to join a Yorkshire regiment where his life was made miserable by the quick-witted Yorkshire men to whom his

Hampshire accent and slow country ways were a source of endless merriment.

Bluebell eyed me coldly that evening and aimed a succession of cow-kicks at me as I tried to get myself, the bucket and the milking stool up to her udder. Several painful weeks passed before she accepted me as part of her war-effort.

Mrs. Dowling, to my mother's dismay, left to do her war work in a munitions factory. I imagined her at the production line deftly turning out shell cases as light and airy as the cheese straws and millesfeuilles that she had made for the pre-war dinner parties.

Although my parents had never been rich, from their earliest married days they had always kept at least three servants – a cook, two maids and when my sister and I came along, a Nanny as well.

I remembered hearing Nanny discussing Myra with the cook in South Eaton Place, before we left London and moved to Litchfield. "Head in the clouds, that one," she said wistfully, "I wouldn't trust her to even boil an egg."

Which was true. She never had had to do any cooking. She did not even like thinking about food, and planning the meals had always been left to Mrs. Dowling. Now a replacement had to be found if we were not to starve to death.

All the domestic servants' employment agencies had closed down because of the war. Eventually a couple called Beavis turned up, refugees from the bombing in the East End of London. When I saw them I had a suspicion that they had come from the same Prisoners Aid Society, which had produced Wilput, the drunken butler.

A cottage was found for them on the Overton Road. Mr. Beavis was a tiny little man who could easily have been a cat burglar; he was supposed to do some gardening, but he seldom left the cottage. Mrs. Beavis was about three times his size. In the mornings she would stump up the back stairs and along the passage to where my mother was having breakfast in bed, war or no war, and stand there with her huge red face and massive frame waiting for orders.

My mother cowered behind her tray, her brow furrowed with the distasteful task. It was very difficult. Although we had our own eggs and milk, chickens, fruit and vegetables, everything else was rationed, and very small rations at that.

One day, after a long silence, Mrs. Beavis made a suggestion. "How about a nice Toad? We've got them sausages from last week." The Beavis' had to go.

Jessie volunteered to do some cooking, although she was no better at it than my mother. Two young girls, both very tall and thin, were found to help her. In the pantry there was a large board tacked to the wall where the shopping list could be chalked, with WANTED written across the top.

The girls did not settle down and soon disappeared after writing on the shopping board, under WANTED:

One Parlour Maid

One House Maid

The Ministry of Food produced a book called the ABC of Cookery and my mother bought one for a shilling. There were long lists of kitchen utensils and diagrams of tablespoons and cheese graters as well as explanations of cooking terms such as baking, beating, glazing, grilling and creaming fat. It could have been written for her.

She and Jessie poured over the chapter on eggs. 'How to Boil Shell Eggs' was helpful, but the drawing on the opposite page of an about-to-be poached egg sliding off a saucer into a pan of boiling water made my mother feel sick. In the poultry section were instructions on cleaning giblets and scalding chicken's feet. They decided on Bovril sandwiches for lunch.

The next cook was another cockney called Mrs. Harris

The next cook was another cockney called Mrs. Harris. She was a chain-smoker with a very white face and very black hair, and a dreadful daughter aged about six called Beryl.

"Tike your feet out of the sink when Madam's talking!" she would scream at Beryl; for now my mother came down to the kitchen mid-morning to order the meals. When she was not paddling in the sink among the potato peelings, Beryl sat on the servants' lavatory under the backstairs with the door open shouting: 'Finished!' while her mother smoked away at the kitchen table telling Mrs. Kilmaster the story of her life. Mrs. Dowling's spotless sanctuary soon became an awful mess.

"I suppose we're lucky to have found her," sighed my mother. "I just wish she wouldn't play the wireless quite so loudly all the time. And it would be nice if she were a better cook."

Imogen was home for half-term. "I don't think we'll have to suffer her for very long. Have you seen the saucepans? We'll all soon be dead of food poisoning."

"You really do make the most unhelpful remarks, darling," said my mother. "I suppose it's your age."

There did not seem to be a Mr. Harris, if there ever had been, but Mrs. Harris had a boyfriend who was in the Army. When he was coming home on leave he would send her exciting telegrams, which made her smoke more and cook less. One of them was opened by my mother by mistake: 'Meet you top of tube, love Bert,' it said. We wondered if she knew which Underground Station he meant.

"Let's hope she falls under a train," said Imogen spitefully.

I was all for Bert coming home on leave; it meant that we would be free of Mrs. Harris and Beryl for at least forty-eight hours.

There were all sorts of fiddles you could do to increase the meagre rations and my mother soon got her head out of the clouds and became an expert. Her first venture, however, was to prove nearly fatal. If you kept bees The Ministry of Food provided extra sugar, albeit rather coarse, and so some hives were procured and put in the orchard amongst the clover and apple blossom. By leaving them some of their combs we felt justified in eating their sugar. The problem was to persuade the bees to go into the hives. Hours were spent banging tin trays as they swarmed merrily all over the garden and in the taller trees.

One day as my mother walked past the orchard a wayward Queen must have settled on her, for in a minute she was the centre of a raging cloud. She began to run, but the bees followed her wherever she went and she was very badly stung. She blew up like a balloon and when she finally shook them off she had to immerse herself in a soda bath.

"Well, I certainly shan't get rheumatism when I'm older," she said when she recovered; unfortunately this proved to be a fallacy. I wondered whether it was worth going through all that agony for some extra sugar.

Our cousin Francis, the famous aviator who was now producing astro-navigational manuals for the Air Force, came to stay. He kept bees in the top floor of his house in St. James's Place in London and seemed to have a great affinity with them. He even let them crawl about on his head inside his hat, which gave me the shudders. While we dressed up in long gloves and huge hats with veils to take the honey he gave them a puff from the smoker and did it in shirtsleeves. One year he sent a pot of honey to the King just down the road; after all, his bees had been plundering the Royal lime trees all summer.

After his visit we regained some of our confidence, but our mother was always afraid of them.

We were also allowed extra petrol coupons because we pumped our own water; by economising on water, which was no problem for me, we could use them for the car. On every station hoarding was the accusation:

'IS YOUR JOURNEY REALLY NECESSARY?'

My mother reasoned that fetching her husband from the station every week was absolutely vital to the war effort.

The parents had an illicit source of much-needed alcohol. A butcher in Whitchurch provided under the counter whisky if you bought your meat from him. It cost a bit on the Black Market, but it was worth it to them. The snag was that you were supposed to exchange your meat coupons with the local butcher with whom you were registered, which in our case was in Overton.

A lot of village people left behind by the war had little else to do except poke their noses into other people's affairs. My mother became a bag of nerves. Once, having forgotten that she had asked PC Harris, the local policeman, to come up to the house to collect some pears (of which we had a great many that year) she screamed with fright when he crept up on her in the orchard, saying " 'Ello, 'ello, wot 'ave we 'ere," as a joke.

Imogen found a way of making butter out of Bluebell's milk, with the help of the flywheel on the water pump, that proved almost as dangerous as our mother's bee-keeping adventures. We certainly needed extra butter rations for the rapacious appetites of the Army friends, and making it by hand was a laborious business. Sitting on an unstable pile of telephone books with the churn clamped between her knees, Imogen fixed the handle to the flywheel and set the machine in motion. As the big webbing belt dashed up and down, the flywheel revolved at great speed and a pound or so of butter was made in minutes.

As usual when either of his children showed some inventive ability our father took the credit. "Takes after me, of course," he said proudly. "Perhaps she should go to University and study engineering. What d'you think, darling? What d'you think?"

"I think it's brilliant," agreed our mother.

It certainly was an effective way of making butter, but you needed nerves of steel. When I tried, the churn soon flew out of my hands and knees and made several circuits of the pump room in mid-air, threatening to kill us, and spewing a stream of curds all over the machinery and ourselves before crashing to the ground.

"I told you to hang on tight, you silly ass!" Imogen berated me through a mask of buttermilk.

After that the job was left to the inventor.

Now that the household was running fairly smoothly my mother decided to join the Observer Corps. My father took a photograph of her wearing her uniform for the first time, standing by the front door, which had been the background for so many glamorous group shots before the war. She is looking a little shyly away from the camera; she always hated being photographed. The baggy blue-grey battle-dress does little for her elegant figure and her hair is swept back from her forehead in a forties' style roll - a long way from the youthful pre-war bob.

She refused to wear her beret for the photograph, but in the early mornings when she wobbled off to her Observer post on an old bicycle, she pulled it well down against the wind and rain. After several spills, when her trouser legs got caught up in the chain, she got some bicycle clips as well. I didn't remember her ever riding a bike in peacetime.

The post was a cunningly camouflaged bunker on a hill above Overton with a field telephone on which my mother learned to say, "Roger, over and out," and a Primus stove for making tea. There she would do four-hour shifts, staring at the skies through my father's race-glasses and gossiping with her mate, who was, in succession, Mr. Stevens, the owner of Overton Motors and Mr. Sharp the chemist.

Mr. Stevens was a nervous type with a mine of false invasion rumours. "They've landed in Kent," he would say, climbing down into the bunker and slipping off his gas mask bag. "They'll be landing in London by dinner-time."

He was, also, a horseracing enthusiast and was more reliable with his tips for the little racing that still survived.

Mr. Sharp had dealt in cosmetics in his shop before the war and, now that they were no longer available, he had useful hints as to how my mother should take care of her complexion.

"He says I should splash my face with butter-milk and drink lots of cabbage water," she told us when she got home, or was it the other way round?

She was given a pack of cards showing the silhouettes of allied and enemy aeroplanes to help her identify them. In the evening we played Observer Corps snap with them in the hall. You had to say the name of the aeroplane on the card (luckily there were several duplicates) before you slapped it down on the table. The mantle of the Aladdin Lamp trembled in the middle of the table, and the room reverberated to shouts of 'Spitfire!' 'Typhoon!' 'Wellington!' and the more tongue twisting German ones, such as 'Focke-Wolf' and 'Messerschmidt'. These last Woman Observer Chichester had not so far been called upon to identify, to her daughter's disappointment.

Chapter Two

Mr. Delitz, our resident artist, had been persuaded to stay on after his usual departure date in late summer. It would be much better for him to spend the war with us than being bombed to pieces in London. A gas stove and black-out curtains were found for the barn and he seemed happily ensconced there. We were surprised, therefore, when he appeared in the garden, one day, where my mother and I were dutifully lifting the dahlias. He was dressed in a long loden-cloth overcoat and a green Tyrolean hat with a bit of fur sticking up at the back. I had never seen him in these clothes before.

"I have some terrible news," he announced in a broken voice. "The boys have been rounded up as Enemy Aliens. Imagine! They were born here! Ach, the evil influence of Adolf Hitler is spreading everywhere." He took off his spectacles and mopped his eyes with one of his paint rags. "I have heard from Fritzi that they are being held in a transit camp in Essex. I must go at once to see if I can stop them going behind the wire."

"But Leo!" My mother jumped up and went to him. I sat back on my heels holding the trowel, the awful phrase 'behind the wire' ringing in my ears. "Won't they pick you up as well? Surely you are taking an awful risk?"

"My dear Myra, I have lived in this country for nearly twenty years. I am not young any more and I do not think I can be considered a threat to the security of the British Isles – with my eyes I can hardly read the telephone book, let alone decipher the secret messages of spies. Anyway, I am prepared. It can be very cold in those camps." The old man patted the warm stuff on his coat. "May I telephone for a taxi?"

Mr. Crutch, the taxi driver from Overton who had black market petrol coupons, came bumping up 'the drive, approach or puddled way'. We all embraced. Mr. Delitz's cheeks were wet with tears. "Goodbye, my dears, think of me and pray for us all. And, little Jane, take care of the pig."

Then he was gone. It had all happened so quickly that my mother and I were stunned. The real sadness came later when we heard from Fritzi (who was a British citizen) that he had indeed been interned with his sons, as my mother had feared. They spent the next two years of the war in a camp on the Isle of Man.

Although my parents tried to justify this cruel treatment of an old man, by saying that a great many dangerous Germans would also have been swept up in the internment net, the incarceration of Mr. Delitz made a profound impression on me. This was real war, not the war I played at in my games.

So now there was the cow to milk, and the ponies to exercise and look after, and the pig to be given his daily bucket of depleted wartime swill. I did not take him for walks. Mrs. Harris and Beryl took a rare turn round the garden, and came and stared at me as I watched Robinson IV snuffling in his bucket, grunting happily, his ears covered with slime. "Wot's that great big 'orrible beast for then?" asked Beryl, picking her nose.

"It's a pig. It's for us to eat when he's big enough, aren't you, Robinson?" I said and I scratched his back with a twig.

"Poor fing," Beryl looked at him sadly.

"Well, you won't catch me cooking it, that's for sure," Mrs. Harris sniffed. "The very idea!" When the time came, the pig had to be taken down to the butchers in Overton, and chopped up and boiled with all the other neighbourhood pigs. We were only allowed to keep half, and it certainly tasted different from Mrs. Dowling's fragrant hams, gammon and brawn.

With all the chores there was little time left over for my education. Robin and I had to gallop between Milcheldever and Deane to fit the lessons in, conjugating Latin verbs and humming piano pieces as we went.

Luckily Robin was now very fit. To help out with the petrol ration, and after some reluctance on his part, we'd taught him how to pull a cart.

Mr. Ranger sold us a rickety old trap that he had in his yard. Vince patched it up, and I painted it red with yellow wheels and bits of green where the paint ran out. It looked very smart when it was finished, but not to Robin. He accepted the shiny harness and blinkers with no trouble, but when shown the multi-coloured trap he backed away. Nothing convinced him to come within feet of the hostile contraption.

"You'll 'ave to start him slow, like," said Vince. "Get 'im used to the idea. We'll try 'im with a log on behind."

For the next few days I harnessed Robin to a four-foot log and made him drag it up and down through the orchard, along the sandy track that lead to the vegetable garden. It was a hazardous business. At first he tried to kill both me and the log: bolting as fast as he could with me flying behind hanging onto the reins, and the log thumping from side to side. The dogs ran with us, barking wildly, and Vince stood watching, wheezing with laughter.

When he had settled down a bit I presented the trap to Robin again and suddenly he decided to become a well-behaved carriage horse. Of course, there were lapses into his normal galloping ways, which I did not discourage. I revelled in this form of transport, charging up and down the drive like Boadicea in her chariot; using any excuse to run errands to the cottages or the crossroads two miles away, where our newspapers were left in a little box tacked to a tree.

"They'll never take him for the Front Line now," I told Vince, as we jingled back to the stables.

"Reckon they won't; 'e's doing vital work on the 'ome front now, 'e's a good little chap," and he rubbed Robin's nose with his fist.

It was a great relief to both of us.

It was also a relief to me when Bluebell, the cow, went dry. I led her down to the farm to be married to Bertie, the Bull. She minced along like a young bride, taking dainty little running steps and pretending to butt me with her horns. This was obviously the highlight of her year.

In the empty farmyard Mr. Ranger eyed me coldly. All the sons, except Donald with the squint, had gone off to war. "You got rid of all them furriners up at the Grange yet?" he asked.

"If you mean Mr. Delitz and the maids," I replied, equally coolly, "yes, they've gone. We miss them very much."

"Aargh." He spat on the ground. Bluebell fluttered her eyelashes, looking around for Bertie. "Bunch of rotten spies, if you ask me."

"I'll fetch her next week." I handed the cow over and ran all the way home. How could anyone call dear old Mr. Delitz a rotten spy? I hated Mr. Ranger.

I did not have to go to Steventon for French lessons any more. The Armstrong's Mam'selle seemed to have disappeared; perhaps she, too, had been interned.

In the spring another 'furriner' turned up. He was a very thin young Norwegian called Gabriel Smith, known as 'Gib', who had escaped from the Germans by sailing a small boat across the North Sea with only a compass and a school atlas to guide him. My parents were friends of his family, and after landing in Scotland he had found his way down to us in Hampshire. He was a pilot and a parachutist, and thought only of joining the Commandos and being dropped back into Norway to help his people. Apart from my father, he was the best looking man I had ever seen, and in the short time he was with us I followed him about like a shadow.

When he was not telephoning his contacts in London, Gib helped Vince split logs in the woodshed wielding the axe like a knight with a sword. I watched, seeing him in my mind's eye as one of my heroes: Siegfried the Dragon Slayer, wearing a gold helmet and slaying his enemies with easy nonchalance.

In reality, he was wearing an old blue shirt and a pair of grey flannel trousers of my father's, as his own clothes had been ripped to shreds in the terrible crossing.

He put the axe down and mopped his forehead, pushing back his straw coloured hair. "I wish you would not keep watching me like that," he said in his slightly whiny singsong English, for like all Scandinavians, including Karin, his voice seemed to come from the back of his nose. "You make me nervous. I will probably cut off my foot."

"Sorry." Reluctantly I took my eyes off him.

"I reckon that ole North Sea gave you a rough time, then," put in Vince, whose admiration for the young man was almost as great as mine. "Them waves 'n all."

"Not so bad; I have been sailing since a boy. The worst was when I reached the Scottish coast. Remember, I had no charts, I did not know exactly where I was."

"Was it a dark and stormy night?" I asked eagerly.

"Yes it was," he looked past me with his wide apart blue eyes, as if he could still see the scene. "And it was very rough, with many jagged rocks. In the end a life boat found me and towed me in."

"Thank heavens for that!" I exclaimed.

"Well, it was a mixed blessing. When they had beached my little boat they took everything I had: my wallet, my watch, which had been my father's, and even the letters I had brought from Norwegians to post to their friends in England."

"I reckon they thought you was a spy, then," said Vince who was a staunch supporter of the RNLI.

"And they gave everything back when they found that you weren't?"

"I'm afraid they did not."

Gib picked up the axe again and flexed his muscles.

"In time of war people can behave strangely, not like their normal selves," he went on, lining up a huge apple stump, "and anyway, they did save my life."

He whirled the blade over his head and brought it down with a crack that split the stump neatly in half, exposing the pinkish grain within.

Later he spent two more leaves with us between sorties over enemy-occupied Norway, each time becoming more silent and withdrawn. Finally he got his wish, being dropped into the mountains to take part in a Commando raid on a German troop train. The mission was successful, but many lives were lost, including his own. He was just twenty-one, eleven years older than me. To Vince and myself his was the only one that mattered. My beautiful Gib.

Molins Machine Company in Deptford, where my father spent most of his working life, switched from producing packets of cigarettes to making ball bearings and other parts for the war effort. Once the Germans started bombing London and the docks in earnest, Marcus was driven to his office every morning through the smoking ruins of the previous night's raid.

We were all relieved when he went off to deliver some vital part to a distant factory in Cornwall or Yorkshire, but that, too, could prove hazardous. All the signposts had been removed to baffle the Germans when and if they did invade us. It was no joke being lost on Ikley Moor in the middle of the night searching for a camouflaged factory. For, by this time, everyone was suspicious of strangers. If my father stopped to ask the way at some isolated farmhouse he had to run the gamut of furious dogs and the owner brandishing a twelve-bore. However, something good did come from one of these excursions. Lost again on the way to some remote destination he pulled up at a house belonging to two old ladies.

They were not interested in ball bearings or spies, and asked him in for a cup of tea. Snug in their basket by the Aga was a litter of Shetland sheepdog puppies. One in particular, a little honey-coloured bitch with a white tip to her tail, made a great fuss of him. Of course he bought her before continuing his journey, and that was how Imogen came by her dog Cherry.

Back at Litchfield, Fred was delighted to have someone his own size to play with, not realising how much bigger she would soon become. As for my sister, the scar left by Brora's death at last began to heal.

One Sunday morning as we sat at breakfast, far away from the horrors of war, our mother dropped a bombshell of her own. "I've invited the Leggatts to come and live with us."

"To live?" I asked. People usually just came to stay. "How long for?"

"Well," replied our mother hesitantly, looking down the table to where our father sat, in his dressing gown, reading the newspaper. "Probably for the duration."

"Gosh," said Imogen. "There was one war that lasted for a hundred years. Not that I don't like the cousins," she added as our mother glared at her.

"What are you talking about, darling? Have they been bombed out or something?"

"Not yet. But I've heard from Dibby. She is so worried with Claud being at the Admiralty and never able to get home, and all the air raids on Bristol getting worse every day. You know they're not very far from Bristol."

"Yes, I know they're not very far from Bristol."

"There would be lots of advantages. We could pool our ration books. And as the house would be full we wouldn't have to have any ghastly evacuees. And it would be fun for the children, they're all the same age."

"How can two children be the same age as four?" asked Imogen. "It's not as if the Leggatts are nothing but twins."

"Don't be tiresome, darling, you know very well what I mean."

"Where will they sleep?" I was beginning to be seriously worried.

"Oh, there's plenty of room. The grown-ups can have the double spare room, the little ones can have the blue room, and we'll put extra beds in with you two for Gilly and Julia."

"No!" Imogen and I expostulated. Our bedrooms were sacrosanct. The thought of sharing them was intolerable.

"We all have to make sacrifices in wartime, darlings. Think of Poland. Think of homeless refugees all over the world."

"But the Leggatts have got a home."

"I shall sleep in the barn."

"The rats will chew your toes."

"I don't care."

Our father put down his newspaper and lit a cigarette. "In these troubled times, as I dodge the bombs in London or dive around the country trying to persuade the locals that I am not a German spy and that I really do want to find the way to Piddle Trenthide, I am sustained by the thought of my peaceful Sunday breakfast in the bosom of my family. Now, will that bosom please shut up or go away?"

We were all silent for a moment.

Then Mrs. Harris slid back the hatch with a bang, stuck her head through it and bellowed: " 'Aven't yer finished yer breakfast yet? And by the way, Mrs. C, I don't know what yer goin' to 'ave for yer dinner. Them fowls that came yesterday is off."

"I'll be along to see you in a minute, Mrs. Harris," our mother said wearily. "Children, clear away, will you?" Mrs. Harris's head withdrew as Imogen and I began to stack the plates.

"I thought she was supposed to call you 'Madam'," said my sister.

"Well, she doesn't any more. There's a – "

And we all took up the familiar refrain and chorused "WAR ON!"

"Children! Go away!" shouted our father, who rarely raised his voice. Mrs. Harris's noisy ways seemed to be catching.

As we reluctantly left the room our mother returned to her theme, "And another thing, darling –"

"Can't it wait till lunch time? Why wreck just one meal a day?"

"You're being very unreasonable. I was just going to say that I thought Claud could share the flat in London with you during the week, he's been given such an awful little room at the Admiralty. And then you could both come down together at weekends."

"It's a very small flat."

"He's a very small man."

The Leggatts arrived at the beginning of the summer holidays. Apart from the Aunt and Uncle there were the four daughters, two hamsters, some white mice, a Norwich terrier and a great deal of luggage. I was not one of the welcoming party.

I watched their arrival through the cracked window of my den in the barn, with much the same sentiments that I imagined the citizens of Eastern Europe felt as the Nazis tramped over their bodies. My private territory was being invaded; nothing would ever be quite the same again.

During the last few days I had seen the house turned upside down to accommodate the invaders. The elegant drawing room, which we hardly ever used, became the children's playroom, or schoolroom if the threat of a governess to give the younger children (which included me) lessons was realised. Drawers were emptied to make room for their clothes, and extra beds and cots crammed into the bedrooms, including mine, the smallest room in the house, for them to sleep on.

On the Sunday after their arrival we all went to Steventon Church as usual, but this time we filled two pews. As I stood beside Julia, sharing a hymnbook, I could feel Miranda Armstrong's curiosity boring into my backbone. Indeed, covert glances were cast at us from all sides of the small congregation.

Afterwards, outside in the graveyard under the yew tree, Miranda took me aside. "What are all those people? Evacuees?"

"No," I answered. "Refugees. They were being terribly persecuted by the Germans so they've fled to us for safety. We had to take them in. They've suffered dreadful hardships and nearly starved to death on the way here."

"Gosh," said Miranda, opening her eyes wide. "Will they stay for long? Do they speak English?"

"Only a few words. It's a bit of a strain, really, having to translate everything. They'll probably stay till the end of the war, they haven't got anywhere else to go."

"Well, I think it's jolly nice of you to have them." Miranda looked at me with new respect.

"It was the least we could do under the circumstances," I sighed valiantly, shrugging my shoulders.

"Jane darling," called my mother from the other side of the yew tree. "Come and introduce Miranda to your cousin Julia."

"Stupid," hissed Miranda, kicking me. "Refugees indeed, 'starving to death, can't speak English'. I thought they didn't look very thin. I'd have been bound to find out, sooner or later."

At lunch our father made a welcoming speech to the Leggatts. He liked doing that sort of thing. He flourished the carving knife and fork over the Sunday joint, and called for silence.

"Welcome one and welcome all," he cried, looking down the rows of expectant faces ranged on either side of the long table. "I hope you will be happy here and consider Litchfield your second home. Please address any complaints to the Manageress. May God bless us all and help us to live in peace and serenity together." His eye dwelt on me for a moment before he plunged the fork into the leg of lamb, releasing a thin pink trickle.

At the other end of the table Uncle Claud, holding a glass of beer, rose to his feet. He was a small man who had been bald for so long the top of his head had turned a deep nut-brown colour to match his face. He said in his deep voice: "On behalf of the residents I would like to thank the Management of this excellent Boarding House for their splendid hospitality. Children raise your glasses. Three cheers for the Chichesters! Hip, hip, hooray!"

The four Leggatt children cheered loud and long. I wished they would stop it. Then Caroline dropped her mug of barley water, and I was sent off to fetch a cloth to mop up the mess. In their corner our dogs wagged their tails at the unaccustomed commotion. Mr. Brown, the Leggatt's dog who had already got the upper hand, snarled at them, defying them to break ranks.

After lunch we were sent out into the garden to play.

"I'm sure cousin Jane has got lots of lovely things to show you," said Aunt Dibby.

Cousin Jane hadn't. Cousin Jane wanted to creep off on her own to her den in the barn or to the safety of the crow's nest in the ship, hidden among the deep green leaves.

The Legatts followed.

"Why are you up at the top of that tree? Can we come, too?"

"Why are you climbing that ladder in the barn? Can we come, too?"

"Where are you going now? Are you going for a ride on your pony? Can we come, too?"

This was to be the pattern of our days. One night as I lay rigid with misery in my bed, thinking of the wonderful days of freedom that I enjoyed this time last year, Julia's voice came from the other bed in my room. "Are you awake?"

"Yes."

"You don't like us being here, do you? Do you wish we hadn't come?"

"Yes." I realised immediately that I had said something very cruel and hurtful; but I didn't take it back. I had said it and I had meant it.

Chapter Three

Karin came to stay, very blonde and beautiful and glowing with young motherhood. Together we pushed her baby daughter Angie down the drive in her pram.

"Ach, these puddles!" cried Karin. "When will they ever be mended?" The baby crowed with delight as the pram bounced over the uneven ground.

"After the war, like everything else," I replied gloomily.

Karin looked round at me. "Mummy tells me that you are being very beastly to your cousins. It is horrid of you, darling; you must not run away and leave them alone all the time."

"They're not alone. They've got each other."

"Yook!" cried Angie, pointing imperiously at the cows in the field. She had big brown eyes and almost white baby hair, and looked like a doll.

"Remember that they have left their own home far away while you are still in yours. You could at least make them feel welcome."

"They've ruined everything; whatever I want to do, they want to do as well. I wish there wasn't a war on. I wish everything was the same as it used to be when I was young." I kicked a pebble along the drive and Fred ran after it and brought it back.

"We all wish the war would go away," said Karin, turning the pram at the end of the drive and starting back towards the house, lying white and serene at the other end. "Just imagine what it is like for me, when Derek goes off in the morning to the airfield to fly sorties over Germany or wherever; Angie and I have to sit alone all day, not knowing whether we will see him again. All the time, all over the world, young men are losing their lives fighting for freedom, and you are grumbling about a few extra cousins coming to live with you! Now that you are so old, my darling, you should be able to appreciate that.

I climbed up the rope ladder to the first big branch

In the morning I made an effort to be nicer. I lined up the three youngest Leggatts under the sycamore tree.

"This is the good ship Dalasenus," I said. "She has already been torpedoed once, but she survived owing to the bravery of her Captain. She is a sleek grey Destroyer, one of the fastest in the Navy, and you are the crew."

"Can I be the Captain?" asked Susan in her deep voice.

"No." I was not prepared to be that nice. "I am the Captain. Julia is the Mate, you are an able seaman and Caroline can be the cabin boy."

I was wearing my beloved rating's cap that my cousin Dick had given me. I had found various nautical-looking gear from the dressing up box for the others to wear.

"Your hat doesn't look like a Captain's hat, it looks more like an able seaman's," observed Julia.

"Never mind. I'm the Captain and you have to obey my orders. All hands on deck!"

I climbed up the rope ladder to the first big branch. Julia and Susan followed slowly as the ladder swung to and fro. I paced the deck impatiently. Caroline stood at the bottom, looking up. "I can't do it, I'll fall off and hurt myself."

"See that man has twenty lashes for disobeying orders, Mr. Mate," I told Julia.

"Must I really? She's only little."

"All right, then. We'll deal with him later. Now, there's a battle coming up. Man the guns, me hearties! Do you see the enemy, Mr. Mate?" I held my telescope, a short piece of lead piping I had found years ago behind the barn, to my eye.

"No," said Julia. I handed her the telescope. She squinted through it into the leaves. "As a matter of fact I feel a bit dizzy."

"I want to go potty!" shouted Caroline from below.

"Well, go then! We're in the middle of a battle, up here. Able-seaman Leggatt, get ready to fire."

"Fire what?" asked Susan, who was sitting on a branch, holding tight.

"Why, the guns, of course!"

"But I want to go properly!" cried Caroline. We looked down at her small figure and saw that she was twisting her legs round each other.

"Run back to the house, then," called Julia.

"Will you come with me? I can't go by myself!"

"Fire!" I shouted at Susan.

"Bang – missed. Bang – missed. Bang – missed." said Susan mildly, pointing her finger towards the tennis court like a toy pistol.

"Why do you keep missing, A B Leggatt?" I asked, genuinely interested.

"Because I'm a rotten shot, Sir," she replied. She did in fact wear glasses.

"Right," I said. "You can go to the sick bay, you're mortally wounded. Mr. Mate, you take over the guns. Ready? Fire!"

"Bang," said Julia languidly. "Actually, I think this is boring. I'm going to go and see to Caroline."

"So am I," said Susan.

They began to climb down through the branches.

"I'll have you all keel-hauled for mutiny!" I shouted after them.

"We don't care!" called back Julia. "Come on, Caroline, let's get away from this silly old tree."

In spite of Karin's words, the cousins did not seem too unhappy about their forcible uprooting, and soon settled down and resumed the childish routine that they had enjoyed at home. And I had to be part of it. I did not consider myself a child. A Lone Ranger, an Outlaw, a Naval Hero, a ferreter, a novelist, but never a child, and routine was abhorrent to me. I had always had an easy-going relationship with the grown-ups, but now we were divided into us and them. Rules were imposed for the children, which I flouted.

But Julia missed her friends that she had left behind in the village, and also the easy access to the sweet shop and the recreation ground.

"Why do you live so far away from anywhere?" she asked.

"Because we like it that way," I replied.

My boundless acres and earthy pursuits did not interest her. One day she did appear at the cow-shed door, and standing there she watched me, sitting on my milking stool, pulling Bluebell's grainy teats, making the jets of milk sing against the side of the pail.

"How disgusting," she said, and went away.

My sleepwalking upset her. She said it gave her the creeps to wake in the middle of the night, and find me with my eyes tight shut standing up against the wall or trying to get into the cupboard. I was rather hurt by her lack of sympathy; I didn't like sleepwalking either, but I couldn't stop it.

They would have liked to have ridden Robin or been taken for jaunts in the trap, but he was shut up in his stable, on a starvation diet, suffering from Laminitis.

"If they're going to stay for a hundred years," I told Imogen, "we'd better get some more ponies."

I went and found my old friend Vince in the kitchen garden. He was lifting the big brown-skinned onions and laying them out on the wire racks to dry, as Mr. Kilmaster used to do before he went off to the war.

"Why, if it isn't her ladyship," He pulled the stained Woodbine out from among his moustaches. "I reckon you'll be havin' a good time, like, with all them pretty little cousins to play with. You needed a bit of company; you always was a loner."

"I still am! But do you know that now, counting Mrs. Harris and Beryl, we've got eleven females living in the house! Can you imagine? And there's this awful routine. It's always time for something: time for meals, time for baths, time to go to bed, just like some blooming institution. What am I to do?" I paused for breath. "Can I come and live with you? I'm not having a good time at all."

The old man laughed and shook the earth off a couple of onions that he was holding by their long yellowish green tops. "I don't know as you'd like that, your ladyship. We ain't got no water closet nor none of them fancy things you're used to. But I tell 'ee what, you bring Fanny over 'ome after dinner and we'll go an' 'ave a look-see for them rabbits in the spinney. We could 'ave a drop of tea and a game of dominoes after, Mother'd be pleased as Punch to see 'ee."

It sounded like heaven.

"I can't, Sir Charles; I'm supposed to be going on a stupid picnic and pick stupid blackberries. See what I mean? My life is no longer my own."

My old friend took off his cap and looked inside it as if seeking inspiration. "Well, I dunno. It could be worse. You could 'ave them evacuees."

"We have!" I cried.

The two eldest, Imogen and Gilly, were getting on better than the rest of us. They were already friends from being at boarding school together, and had grown-up talks about ST's and B squares which meant nothing to me. Gilly was the Leggatt's half-sister and the reason for the break-up of her mother's first marriage.

She was built on a big scale, like Imogen, and had a strong character. She would not have allowed her parents to harass her and tell her to stop poking her head.

Sometimes she went too far. One day the terrier, Mr. Brown, was chasing our Muscovy ducks – a wicked habit that he had brought with him from Somerset and in which our dogs never indulged – and Gilly decided to stop him. Round and round the house she ran, shouting and yelling and chasing the dog that was chasing the ducks.

Muscovys are slow movers at the best of times, with their cumbersome bodies and clipped wings. The dog barked, enjoying the fun, and the ducks quacked and squawked, shaking their red wattles in terror. By the time Gilly had got hold of Mr. Brown, Shadrack, Meshag and Abednego lay dead from exhaustion.

In London the fathers were also finding cohabitating difficult. Being squashed into a tiny flat without their wives to look after them was a new experience. There were scenes at breakfast when one took too much marmalade or over-did the butter ration on his toast. The blitz was at its height and everyone was short-tempered through lack of sleep.

Many spent nights in the underground tunnels or in Anderson shelters for safety; in Sloane Street the flat dwellers moved their beds into the long interior passages in case the blast from a bomb blew the windows in. There were those who snored, those who coughed and those who cried out in their dreams.

Uncle Claud, a light sleeper, was driven to a frenzy by the racket. He would walk up and down the lines of beds shaking the snorers and forcibly administering Famel Syrup to the coughers. There was nothing he could do about the ones having nightmares. Marcus found it more restful to join the fire fighters on the roof, spotting incendiaries landing on the tops of adjacent houses.

Sometimes in the early morning rush the two men overlapped in the bathroom. One day Uncle Claud made an announcement as he sat soaping himself in the bath. "Fifty-five years ago today, a tiny baby boy was born."

"What? What? Whatever are you talking about?" cried Marcus who was shaving at the basin. "Damn!" He nicked his chin with his razor and drew blood.

"I was only going to say that it's my birthday."

"My dear fellow! Congratulations! Why didn't you tell me?" My father was mortified. That day he did not complain when Uncle Claud had two helpings of marmalade at breakfast.

Claud had a very important job at the Admiralty, sending convoys across the North Sea to Russia. It was a harrowing time as more and more of our ships were sunk by German U Boats. However, a cheerful photograph of him and his staff was taken and, in the form of a 4" x 5" propaganda leaflet, was dropped by the hundred over occupied Europe.

A Belgian friend in the Resistance movement found a stack of them hanging on a nail in some French privy where they were serving a very useful purpose. Claud was rather offended when he found out, many years later, the use to which his face had been put during the war.

I liked the weekends when the fathers came home, re-introducing a male element into our all-female household. For them it was a time of relaxation and catching up on lost sleep. But it was not all peace and harmony among the grown-ups. One Saturday morning, when I went along to my parents' bedroom with the tray of china tea that Jessie had given me, I found my mother alone in the big bed.

"Daddy's in his dressing-room," she said. "You can take his tea in there. I'm probably not going to speak to him today."

"Why ever not?"

"He was very rude to Aunt Dibby at dinner last night. He threw a pot of potted shrimps at her."

"Heavens! Was it full?"

"That's not the point."

Next door my father was sitting up in bed looking tousled, but unrepentant. "Very argumentative woman, your Aunt."

Apart from the occasional personality clash with my father, Aunt Dibby was actually a great help in the present situation. With her large family she was used to running a house full of children, and had tactful ways of dealing with Mrs. Harris and Jessie, which my mother lacked, accustomed as she was to leaving all the culinary decisions to Mrs. Dowling.

The two adult sisters were the ones who enjoyed our new communal life-style the most. They had forged a deep bond of sibling love and loyalty during their extraordinary childhood, but with the enforced separation of their marriages they had not seen so much of each other for years.

They had also experienced the heartache, hardship and food shortages of the First World War together. In their early teens, continuing their meagre education, they had been sent to a convent in North London where the kindly nuns were on the verge of starvation. Although food had never been plentiful at home in Wiltshire where they lived mostly on potatoes and the occasional rabbit, the Jay sisters had never eaten horsemeat until it appeared on the rectory table as a rare treat. Myra, who had always been a sickly child with a queasy digestive system, grew quite ill. The building had hardly changed since the Middle Ages and was bitterly cold.

Their mother, now a penniless widow, had been taken in by the ever kind-hearted Great Aunt, and gone to live in Berkeley Square. When Armistice Day came Dibby and Myra hopped over the wall and ran away down the hill to London to join the ecstatic throng singing and dancing in the streets, finally ending up at Number Twenty-Two expecting a warm welcome. Unfortunately, their reception was cool. The Belvilles were having a dinner party – there were no food shortages there – and the two dishevelled little girls did not fit in. Even their mother was distracted. While the rest of the world rejoiced, she had just received the news that her only son, George, had been killed in France, hours after the Armistice had been signed. Dibby and Myra were put into a taxi and sent back to the Convent in Mill Hill.

The swift introduction of rationing in the Second World War avoided the inequalities of food supply in the first, and nobody starved. But until Aunt Dibby arrived the food at Litchfield was pretty basic. My mother had been given another cookery book, slightly more advanced than the 'ABC', compiled by Gert and Daisy who were a famous pair of comics. After she had suggested to Mrs. Harris that she should make the turnip pie on page six they had not been on speaking terms.

My Aunt soon gained the confidence of the indolent kitchen staff, and had them bottling and pickling, and preserving eggs in isinglass. I remember the taste of dried eggs, resorted to when the hens stopped laying. It was like grated cardboard.

Liquid paraffin in small quantities could be used for making cakes, and the fat off the top of rare tins of sausage meat came in handy for pastry.

The purloined sugar that the bees should have been enjoying went into jam making, as did the ash off the end of Mrs. Harris's cigarette. Both were soon absorbed in the boiling mixture, and Aunt Dibby turned a blind eye: after all, there was a war on.

Mrs. Kilmaster was actually quite good at it all, and lots of washing-up helped to stop her worrying about her husband. For the first time her two horrible daughters, Coral and Sylvia, were allowed to come over the field with her. By my calculations there were now fourteen females in the house at certain times of day.

Knowing that she was leaving the running of the place in good hands, Woman Observer Chichester slung her gas mask and her binoculars over her shoulder and pedalled to her Post. The skies were full of aeroplanes now, some of them hostile and all of them needing spotting; she became an expert at cranking the field telephone and passing on vital information. Much as she was enjoying the company of her sister, these shifts gave her the chance to get away for a few hours from the household full of busy women and noisy children.

I envied her and missed her. For I was the odd one out. Even Aunt Dibby did not know how to deal with me. I was finding it impossible to come to terms with the take-over of my house and my private life, and was becoming rude and intractable. I came in late for meals, dirty and dishevelled. Having washed their hands and combed their hair, the Leggatts would already be sitting, tucking-in.

What was now the 'schoolroom' had become a sort of junior Women's Institute with handicrafts and jigsaw puzzles, knitting and sewing, and board games at the table, which I refused to join. As the visitors settled in and made the place their own I became more and more disenfranchised.

In September, dressed up in Harris Tweed and darned lisle stockings and sensible shoes, Imogen and Gilly went back, quite cheerfully, to their boarding school in the drifting misty rain of Exmoor. At home a governess had been found for Julia, Susan and me.

And this was when my life took a definite turn for the worse.

You would have thought our mothers' experience as children would have put them off governesses forever, but this was not the case. I remonstrated that my education was in the hands of Rev. Hardcastle and the Misses Scutt, but word came from the vicar that now he had joined the Home Guard he was too busy to continue with my lessons. Saddened, I wondered whether he was allowed to wear his Prussian helmet with the splendid imperial eagle when he went out on patrol. At the same time the Misses Scutt reneged; their time was taken up knitting for the troops, as though the Army was already at the gates of Sebastopol.

So Mrs. Carter, a no-nonsense Yorkshire woman with a long body, short legs and a bland expression that missed nothing, arrived to take over our education.

She and I started badly. When she stepped out of the car that brought her from the station I was just sloping round the back of the barn with Fred, looking for rats. "Whatever is that child doing with that gun?" she demanded.

"Oh, that's Jane, our rebel," said Aunt Dibby cheerfully. "Rather a law unto herself, you could say."

"Well, I hope she won't shoot me." She had a trace of Yorkshire in her voice and a way of smiling with her teeth clenched as I found out when I came indoors, late as usual, for our new meal, High Tea.

As alcohol was so scarce during the war the parents kept what little there was for the weekends when the fathers came home. The mothers found their teetotal weekdays a particular strain – no swish of soda into the whisky, no tinkle of ice in the gin and tonic – and instituted High Tea to fill the vacant cocktail hour. There would be some indigestible hot dish like macaroni cheese or baked beans on toast, bread and honey and sometimes a cake.

I found it all a waste of time. High Tea may have taken the mothers' minds off drink, but meanwhile out of doors the end of the day was being

She thinks she's being boyish wearing those dreadful shorts
and keeping all that iron-mongery in her pockets

lost to me. Steel grey night clouds were rolling up on the last flaming banners of the sunset, and partridges called to each other in the ghostly mist rising from the fields. The wild world was going to bed. I was missing the whistle of pigeon coming in to roost, the lonely cry of the hunting owl.

"Pass the honey, Jane," said Julia, bringing me back with a bump. That first evening Mrs. Carter told us all about her previous employers. We were to get to know them well in the weeks to come.

In common with most governesses, the children that she had left behind in her previous post were paragons of virtue, intellectual prowess and physical grace. She had looked after two boys and two girls, Ian and Tom, Phoebe and Sarah. Ian was Mrs. Carter's favourite in this perfect family. He had a brilliant brain as well as beautiful manners, and you would never find him coming to the meal-table with dirty fingernails (unlike some, was the unspoken comment, personally addressed to me).

"I'm afraid you may find our children a bit of a let-down," said my mother. "The Hichens family do sound a hard act to follow."

"I'm ready for t'challenge," said Mrs. Carter.

She came from Barnard Castle, one of the out-posts of Roman Britain, and in the holidays she and her husband tramped along Hadrian's Wall, and took part in archaeological digs. This should have been a bond between us, but it was not. In the schoolroom our general deportment took precedence over our actual education, and there I failed dismally. I became the butt of her Yorkshire wit and sarcastic jibes.

"There are some little girls who seek to deny their birthright and pretend that they are boys," was one of her themes. "I can think of one, right here in this room. A dirty little tyke, too. Can you find her, girls?"

Julia was embarrassed, but Sue shot up her hand. "Jane."

"Quite right, Susan. She thinks she's being boyish by wearing those dreadful shorts and keeping all that iron-mongery in her pockets. It's a wonder she can sit down at all, isn't it, girls?"

I was compared unfavourably with the Hichens family several times a day. "If you were to see my Ian at the crease in his white flannels," she would say, "standing up straight and swiping the ball like a young Greek God, you would realise that there is a difference between a boy and a hobbledehoy."

"I didn't know Greek Gods played cricket," I murmured and got another black mark.

Lessons became an ordeal. We were to start with physical jerks on the lawn. On the first morning Mrs. Carter and the Leggatts carried the ancient wind-up gramophone, with the big horn, out into the garden and stood waiting. I shambled down from the stables with the milk bucket.

"Where have you been? You're late," snapped the governess.

"Milking the cow," I said, preparing to walk on.

"You put that bucket down and come and get in line. Whatever next? Milking the cow, indeed!"

She put the Turkish Patrol on the turntable and lowered the arm.

"Ready – and – one, two, one, two," she cried, jumping up and down flapping her arms in the air like a wounded duck, as the first wheezing notes took the air. Julia and I caught each other's eyes and began to giggle. The dogs joined in, barking madly and rushing around our little group, snapping at our legs. Cherry, Imogen's beautiful Shetland sheepdog, who was full-grown now, put her paws on my shoulders and licked my face. I fell over and we rolled on the grass.

Mrs. Carter took the needle off the record. "This is impossible. Tomorrow, Jane, you can see to it that the dogs are locked up when we do our PE. Now, indoors everybody."

Lock up the dogs? The woman was clearly mad. Later in the day I tried to tell my mother so. We were alone in her bedroom, that light and sunny room at the end of the wing that stood at right angles to the house. Up here you could look down on the stone paved rose garden on one side and across to the long field with its grazing cattle on the other, where Mr. Delitz used to sit sketching under his big umbrella. You could almost forget about the war and the fact that the rest of the house was full of nagging women.

But my mother had just returned from a long tiring shift at the Observer Post and was in no mood to sympathise. "We've all got to adapt in wartime, darling, and I don't think a little discipline will do you any harm. You'll have to milk the cow before breakfast."

"Bluebell won't like it," I said. "She's a creature of habit."

"So is Mrs. Carter, I'm afraid, and she's the boss. If she wants to do half an hour's gym before lessons that's what you'll have to do. She says it stimulates the oxygen supply to the brain."

"I think I've got too much oxygen in my brain already," I grumbled. "Mrs. Carter says I'm extremely backward for my age."

"Well, you'll just have to try to catch up."

I picked up her blue Observer Corps blouse and tried it on, looking at myself in the long triple glass. I had not expected her to take the enemy's side. "Bother Mrs. Carter," I muttered. "Bother the war. Bother everything," and pulled a face at my reflection.

My mother turned round on the stool where she sat at her dressing table doing her hair. She had grown very thin. "I do wish you'd stop being so bolshie, Jane," she said crossly. "It's really not at all helpful. Now run along and see what the others are doing."

The war came closer. On the return journey from a raid on Germany, a crippled Wellington bomber spiralled out of the sky and crashed into a field a few miles away. When I got there I found the cockpit, broken off from the rest of the fuselage by its impact with the ground, lying on its side on the stubble. Inside, next to the instrument panel, where the pilot had been sitting, I saw a half-eaten sandwich.

Villagers were already chopping off bits of the wings and the tail plane and the rear-gunner's turret, to take home as souvenirs. I walked away thinking about the remains of the sandwich: still lying there although the man who had been eating it was dead.

"Where have you been?" asked the others when I got back to the house. "You're late for prep."

Soon afterwards a stray bomb flattened St. Vincent's, the day school in Basingstoke that I had been threatened with long ago. It fell in the middle of the afternoon when nearly all the pupils were out in the playing fields. A sick child and the matron looking after her were the only ones killed, left behind as they were in the main building.

The sound of gunfire could be heard coming from Popham Camp where the Army practised target shooting.

"There they go," said Caroline calmly as Aunt Dibby pushed her in her pram down one of our country lanes. "Sheenmagunnin' again."

Meanwhile, in the schoolroom, hostilities bubbled beneath the surface like lava in the diagrams of volcanoes that Mrs. Carter caused us to draw. My imagination was caught by our geology lessons and the terrifying forces at the centre of the earth that caused earthquakes and volcanic eruptions, but my artwork looked like one of Mrs. Dowling's chocolate puddings with a generous filling of raspberry jam. Julia's was the best with carefully traced cinder cones, lava flows and flank eruptions; but then Julia was best at everything. She was streets ahead of me in arithmetic, and could reel off all thirty-nine books of the Bible with scarcely a pause for breath.

This was the first perfectly useless task of the day after we had finished with the Turkish Patrol. "Genesis, Exodus, Leviticus, Numbers, Deuteronomy, Joshua, Judges, Samuel – er – " I would falter and grind to a halt.

"Ruth," snapped Mrs. Carter. "Whatever happened to Ruth? Lost amid the alien corn again, I suppose. Concentrate, Jane! Your turn, Julia dear."

Julia was also pretty, clean and tidy. She was fast supplanting Phoebe Hichens in Mrs. Carter's affection. I was none of these things. One day, as we worked at 'Composition' the governess paused by my chair and sniffed.

"Don't tell me! You've got that ferret down your shirt again! Wretched child! Take it away!

I leapt at the chance to leave the room and take Fanny back to her cage. Outside the air was fresh and sharp with the first October frost. I was in no hurry to return to the hated schoolroom.

I fetched my 4.10 from the saddle room and took aim at a crow flying overhead. To my astonishment it fell to the ground, stone dead. Filled with remorse, I carried it gingerly round to the pets' cemetery under the chestnut tree and dug a grave. It was a much bigger bird than it had seemed from the ground, shiny and black and somehow evil looking. I felt sorry that I had killed it. There was enough killing going on in the world already.

The shot had been heard down in the house. That evening Mrs. Carter complained about my behaviour to my mother.

"It is not that she lacks ability, Mrs. Chichester," she began. "It is her general attitude that I find so shocking. In all my years as a governess with many different families I have never met a child like her. Don't worry –" My mother's face had obviously dropped and she was expecting the woman to give her notice. "– I will not be defeated. Sooner or later she will learn that life is about conforming to the rules and that she is not some kind of wild mustang that suddenly finds itself herded into the corral."

"Oh dear," said my mother wearily, clearly hankering for a dry Martini. "I suppose it is a bit of a problem. She always has been rather an individualist."

"There's time and a place for individualism, if I may say so. My boys had plenty of character, but they knew how to keep it in check. They were very fond of country sports; Ian, of course was an excellent shot as well as being a first class games player. But they knew where their duty lay when it came to the serious business of daily lessons. You wouldn't find them bringing ferrets into the schoolroom!"

"Forget the ferrets," advised Aunt Dibby who, as I have said, was a practical person. "The trouble with Jane is that she is over-Leggatted, poor darling. Give her time, she'll be all right in the end."

Lurking on the stairs I overheard this conversation. I may have been going to be 'all right in the end' as my dear Aunt had suggested, but the end was nowhere in sight. I had had enough. I decided to run away.

There were two alternatives. I could run away to Southampton and hide below decks on some battleship, emerging far out to sea to play an heroic part in the next encounter with the enemy; or I could go to London and throw myself on the mercy of my father in the Sloane Street flat.

I imagined him opening the door. "Darling! How lovely to see you! Whatever are you doing here?"

"I'm too unhappy at home," I would tell him. "I've come to live with you. I can probably cook your breakfast and be a junior Fire-spotter on the roof," and he would put his arms around me and draw me in.

Both these plans involved catching a train from Micheldever. I could afford the fare as I still had some of the tips the grown-ups had given us before the war in a tin box under my bed. The station was five miles away by road, but much nearer if you went along the railway line, which was just a short distance away across the fields.

I had never actually caught a train by myself or walked along the track, but the railway line had always been something of a magnet to me. In the freedom of my peacetime life I had often lain on top of the embankment in the dark when I was supposed to be in bed, and watched as the trains came flying towards me, trailing their plumes of orange smoke like fiery dragons. The white slopes of the chalky cutting flickered with wild shadows and trembled to the diddley dump, diddley dump of the wheels as the ribbon of steamy windows and lonely silhouettes sped past.

At the mouth of the tunnel down to my right the driver would blast the whistle and then the yellow squares of light would tumble over each other, bouncing off the walls, and be gone. Sometimes sparks from the engine caught the patches of scrub that clung to the embankment, starting small fires that made me think of a soldiers encampment before a battle, huddling round telling stories and keeping warm.

And on summer mornings, very early, Imogen and I had gone down there to gather the wild strawberries that flourished on the chalky slopes, slipping and sliding and taking care not to upset our baskets. It was quiet and peaceful then with larks trilling overhead and any train that came along bore no relation to the fiery dragons of the night.

Now I laid my plans for my escape from what I had begun to think of as The Occupation. I would have liked to have taken Robin and Fred with me, but they would have been frightened by the trains. I had decided that London was the best bet, battle-ships in Southampton docks probably had very tight security. After breakfast, I packed my pyjamas and toothbrush in my gas mask bag, and in the evening asked permission from Mrs. Carter to go to the loo in the middle of prep.

"Why don't you go before, like the others?" she complained.

"I suppose my bladder's weaker."

"Don't be cheeky. Well, run along then, and be quick."

Run along! If she knew where I was running to. And leaving at this time of day no one would think of looking for me for ages. My gas mask was hanging on its peg by the gents. I slung it over my shoulder and slipped out of the house. I already had the money feeling nice and warm in the pocket of my corduroy trousers.

Outside the October evening was turning into night. At the end of the drive I crossed the lane and followed the hedge on the Micheldever side of the two fields between us and the railway line. I did not look back. It would not have done to have had misgivings at this stage.

A wooden fence separated the field from the line and I was quickly over it. My eyes were accustomed to the half-dark and I swung along easily, taking big strides from one sleeper to another, the clinkers between were too sharp for the thin walking shoes I was wearing.

I felt wildly exhilarated by my great adventure… I had got away from that houseful of fussy females! I would strengthen the bond, which I had always had with my father and which had been weakened by this beastly war: nowadays he was so tired at weekends after the incessant bombing in London that he spent most of Saturday and Sunday asleep in his armchair, ignoring me.

The line was running through flat country with familiar fields on either side. Up to the left was the larch wood where my father and I used to go pigeon shooting. I would soon be at Micheldever. No trains so far. Then I heard the whistle of the down train echoing under the tunnel where Vince and his mother lived. I was on the down line. With a bound I leapt off the sleepers, cleared the clinkers and rolled onto the sloping grass bank, the gas mask bag slapping my shoulder.

I never knew trains could go so fast – I had always either watched them from above or got on when they were stationary; you don't get half the impression of speed when you are inside. This one seemed to make the mile from the tunnel in a matter of seconds and suddenly was upon me, roaring by, its wheels pounding just above my head. I clung to tufts of grass to stop myself being sucked under them. One Cyclops light lit the silver rails ahead, otherwise all the carriages were blacked out and even the plume of smoke was only faintly pink. It was like a ghost train slicing through the night.

As suddenly as it had come it was gone, and I could hear it hooting its way through the two tunnels on the approach to the station. Slightly shaken, I picked myself up and resumed my walk along the sleepers. I began to try and remember the ramblings of old Mrs. Vince who knew all the London train times off by heart. 'The eleven thirty were six minutes late today!' I heard her screech. So that was probably the six thirty. Now when was the next up-train? Six forty-two? As if in answer, a far-off whistle came from the first of the Micheldever tunnels and almost immediately, a second blast...

I jumped off the track again, but now instead of a grassy slope I landed on a chalky bank, which was the beginning of the tunnel excavations. I rolled sideways, dangerously near the down line that was thankfully empty, again mesmerised by the hurtling train and pounding wheels. The whole stretch of line vibrated, and I could get no grip on the crumbly chalk. If the train had been on the side where I was lying I could have rolled down into its path.

When the noise had died away and silence returned I got to my feet and took stock. It would take me about ten minutes to get to the mouth of the first tunnel; so that by the time the next train came along I would be safely inside. But a chill thought struck me: how safe would I be inside? Would there be some kind of walkway, a rail to cling onto, a niche to hide in as the monster swept past? The only way to find out was to go and look. We Chichesters were afraid of nothing, I told myself; hadn't we defeated the Armada?

It was completely dark now and difficult to judge the distance between the sleepers. I tripped and fell in mid-strike and banged my knee. It hurt a lot and I could feel something warm trickling down my shin. The chalky banks were shimmering in the darkness, and I hurried on to get to the mouth of the tunnel before the next train came; at least there would be its brick wall to hold on to. I remembered the old nursery rhyme and modified it to suit the occasion:

'Oh look, Mamma, what is that mess that looks like strawberry stain?'

'Hush, hush, my dear, it's cousin Jane, run over by a train.'

I reached the huge black hole of the tunnel's mouth just as the next down train whistled under Vince's cottage. There was a slight recess between the wall and the bank, filled with brambles; I pressed myself into it with a beating heart as the Cyclops eye dashed toward me.

This time I was close enough to the engine driver to see him reach for the cord that pulled the whistle, and for a moment I thought that he had seen me. Then the sheer volume of sound ricocheting off the echoing embrasure engulfed me. Shock waves sent tears rolling down my cheeks and I felt my teeth rattling in my head. It was no joke being quite so near to the speeding London train and I shook like a jelly. When the last of the carriages had whisked past I extricated myself from the brambles and staggered down on to the line.

The taillight bobbing along illuminated the curving walls and I could discern no rail, no recess, no handhold whatsoever, had I been in the tunnel already there would have been nothing to stop me from wobbling under the wheels. As silence returned I heard the steady drip of water. I ran my hand over the nearest wall. It was wet and slimy.

I couldn't do it. Not at night. I could hear my ancestors rattling their sabres in disapproval, but I turned back. I would curl up in some rabbit warren and wait till morning.

On my return journey, I slipped and fell several times, and when I reached the flat bit of country where the field stretched back to Litchfield I was feeling sorry for myself. My knee hurt and I had scratched my hands on the brambles. Limping along, it must have taken me about an hour to reach that point, and I was surprised that there had been no more trains. I was beginning to have doubts about spending the night in the open and decided to sneak home and sleep in one of the long mangers in the loose boxes. I would set off again in the dawn.

Throughout the evening there had been a great hue and cry, with cousins and governess, mother and aunt searching the garden, stables and barn, calling my name. Then the household had given up and gone indoors, and the children had been put to bed. My mother rang the Overton police and reported me as a missing person; Gertie, the one woman telephone exchange, had joined in with the tales of children being abducted in war time and ending up as slave labour in Germany.

The dogs were let out again last thing and this was when Fred with his black button nose, picked up my scent. I had taken one of the ponies' rugs out of the saddle room and, wrapped up in it, was fast asleep in an empty loosebox manger. It was Fred who found me. I woke to hear him yapping outside the door. He was soon joined by the other dogs and then they all rushed in followed by my mother and aunt, with torches.

Sarcasm is a deadly weapon against a child and my mother used it to good effect that night. If she had been seriously worried by my disappearance, as I believe she was, she gave no sign.

"Oh look!" she cried with a false laugh, and began to sing; "Away in a manger, no room for her head, our poor little Janey lay down her sweet head!" in a mocking voice that cut me to the quick. "Let's leave her there, Dibs, she looks perfectly comfortable."

I sat up and blinked in the light of the torch. I must have been an awful sight, hair on end, face and hands dirty and covered in scratches.

"Come on, darling," said Aunt Dibby in her deep, soothing voice, ignoring her sister. "You need a wash and a hot drink." She lifted me out of the manger and down onto the floor. Fred was beside himself with joy, sniffing my trousers and jumping up. I was shivering now and near to tears. I held Aunt Dibby's hand as we walked through the garden following my mother's long striding legs.

In the house she telephoned the police to tell them that I had been found.

"I'm glad to hear it, Ma'am," said PC Harris. "This is no night for a child to be out on her own. There's one hell of a security scare going on down Micheldever."

"Really?"

"Yes. They think there's a German spy loose in them tunnels where the fuel dump is. One of the train drivers spotted him. The Army's turned out to find the blighter – he may be dangerous. They've stopped all the London trains."

"Where were you last night?" asked Julia in the morning. "We had to look for you for hours. It was really boring."

"I just decided to go and sleep in the stables," I said, trying not to look as stiff and sore as I felt.

"Well, you might have told us. The grown-ups were in a fearful fuss, they seemed to think you'd run away."

We got out of bed and started pulling our clothes on in the cold bedroom. Fred began to worry one of my socks. "Was Mummy upset?"

"I should think so, she was the worst of all."

I thought this over, remembering the cool sarcasm with which she had greeted my discovery in the manger.

"And they told us that you were this fragile little flower who had had her space invaded and that we all had to be terribly nice to you if you ever came back." Julia made a rude noise and aimed a pretence punch at my face, I parried with another and we wrestled on the floor. We were friends!

"Did you lay an egg when you was in the manger?" asked Caroline after breakfast. "The bantams would have."

"No," I replied. "There wasn't time," and everybody laughed.

Although no further mention was made of my escapade, for the rest of the day I was treated rather like someone who has just come out of hospital. There was a just-detectable softening of Mrs. Carter's attitude toward me, and no row about my unfinished prep of the previous evening.

In our short free time in the afternoon I repaired to my den in the barn to write up my diary. I concluded a graphic account of my adventure with the words: 'As a matter of fact I'm glad I botched it; I might never have got used to London with all those hard pavements and bombs. And a good thing to come out of it all is that Julia and I have become quite good friends.' I closed the book and put it back in its hiding place under a bale of straw.

No German Spy was ever found, but from then on an armed guard was posted at all the tunnel entrances. It was years before I was able to boast that I had, single-handed, stopped all the London trains for one whole night.

Chapter Four

Having no brothers of my own and only female cousins in our immediate family my knowledge of the opposite sex was negligible. All this was to change in subtle ways in the Spring.

A land girl was billeted on us by the farmer for whom she worked at nearby North Waltham. Although Ruth was not a man, but a strong earthy blonde, well up to the task of feeding Britain, she knew all about men. She had several brothers and, before the war, her father had coached the Cambridge Boat Race crew. Her room was full of photographs of enormous young men in long thin boats, some of them lying in positions of total exhaustion over their oars, others shaking their fists in triumph.

Always cheerful, she had a way of prefacing every remark with a shout of laughter. She went off to work at the farm early each morning on her bicycle, returning in the evening smelling tantalisingly of sweat and diesel oil. I envied her her uniform of khaki shirt, brown corduroy breeches and boots, though not the incongruous pork-pie hat she was supposed to wear on top of her cloud of yellow hair.

My curiosity was aroused by the photographs of the brawny rowers with their bulging muscles and tight shorts. Sometimes when she was out I would steal into her bedroom to look at them. Once I found a letter from a boyfriend lying on the dressing table and read it. There was a lot of soppy stuff and then at the end he asked her a riddle: 'Question: What sticks out of a man's pyjamas that he can hang his hat on?' 'Answer: His head.' I thought it a pretty boring riddle. Perhaps I'd try it on the others at lunch.

In the kitchen Mrs. Harris complained at this addition to the already bursting household. "Another bloody mouth to feed," she grumbled to Mrs. Kilmaster, squashing her cigarette butt into the overflowing ashtray, as they sat at their elevenses at the kitchen table. "And if I know them land girls she'll eat like a bloody horse."

She went off to work at the farm early each morning on her bicycle,

"It'll mean another ration book, though," said Mrs. Kilmaster, showing her pink plastic gums as she munched a biscuit. "At this rate, we ought to have enough coupons for a nice Sunday joint one of these days. How my old man used to love his Sunday dinner! Lord knows what they're feeding him now," she sniffed, close to the tears that were always ready to flow whenever memories of her husband were mentioned.

The fact that his life was not in danger from enemy gunfire at the depot in Yorkshire, where he was servicing Army vehicles, was no comfort to her. "I know he'll go and blow hisself up!" she would cry. "Him not knowing the first thing about engines except for that old Atco lawn mower, bless him."

"It's no good you going on about 'Nice Sunday Joints'," snapped Mrs. Harris, lighting up again. "You'd need half a cow to feed this lot. And tike your fingers out the pig-bucket, Beryl, there's nothing for you in there!"

'Lend a Hand on the Land!' was the army's slogan. Fired with patriotic zeal I suggested to Julia that we should do so, too, even if we were under age. It was a fine spring Saturday and she was sitting sewing in the schoolroom. She was not enthusiastic.

The only time Mr. Ranger let us help on his land was when we brought the tea out for the harvesters, but along the ridge to the west there was a small-holding belonging to Mr. Ravenscroft. He was always short-handed. His wife kept Jacob sheep and mountain goats whose fleece she spun and knitted into hideous garments. In the kitchen there were vats of vegetable dye in various stages of maturity, so that there was little room left over for cooking food.

Their only son had been born deaf and dumb, but early on they had discovered in him a talent for painting and had managed to put him through an Art College in Winchester. As a result he preferred to sit drawing pictures of stooks of corn rather than manhandling them. Before the war I had occasionally done odd jobs there, and been allowed to drive the carthorse while Mr. Ravenscroft loaded up the wagon behind, with the hay and straw lying in the fields. Once at the end of a long hot afternoon he had given me a ten-shilling note.

"Let's go and lend Mr. Ravenscroft a hand," I said to Julia.

"I don't want to. Besides I've got to finish this sewing for Mrs. Carter."

"Once he gave me a ten bob note."

"Oh, well, that's different. Though I can't think what we'd spend it on, stuck out here in the middle of nowhere." She still had a hankering for the cosy proximity of the Wrington village shop, but she did agree to come along to the farm.

We put on our corduroy trousers, tucked into our boots to look like land girls, and aertex shirts. Under Julia's shirt her developing bosom was already showing a couple of points; if that happened to me I had decided that I would cut them off.

We saddled Robin and Thea and rode over to the farm. Crossing the railway bridge by Vince's cottage, trotting through the rabbits' spinney and then cantering along the track between the fields of young winter wheat. The sun shone brightly out of a hazy blue sky, there was the smell of the earth warming up after the long winter, and the sound of twittering birds.

"Yaroo! Here we come, Cassidy!" I cried, tooting my US Cavalry bugle. "Relief is at hand!"

"Who's Cassidy?" panted Julia, trying to control Thea.

"Why, the fellow who has been holding the fort against the Indians all this time. Yaroo! Follow me, men!"

"Actually, I think my postilion's been struck by lightning," said Julia languidly as we slowed up at the entrance to the farmyard.

Mr. Ravenscroft opened the gate for us. He had a grizzled beard and moustache, and wore a felt hat that had known better days. He was dressed like a music hall farmer with a spotted handkerchief round his neck and binder twine gripping his trousers below the knee. A dilettante, my father called him; my mother thought they were gypsies.

"Hello, my dears! To what do I owe the pleasure of this visit?" he enquired.

"We've come to lend a hand," I said dramatically, dismounting from Robin. "We're sort of land girls now. This is my cousin Julia, she's staying with us for the war."

"Is she now?" His bright blue eyes took in Julia's aertex shirt and wavy brown hair. "That'll be a tidy stop, then." Sometimes he affected a proper farmer's way of talking.

"What would you like us to do?"

Wearing one of her homespun garments, Mrs. Ravenscroft was sitting outside the farmhouse milking a goat. She waved to us. "Well, let me see. I've got these two Italian gentlemen supposed to be helping me, but 'dolce far niente' is the order of the day with them, if you ask me. You could go and see what they're up to. They're supposed to be feeding the little calves."

We tied up the ponies and went over to the barn. Inside two dark-skinned, curly-haired young men with sad brown eyes stood leaning against the calf-pens. One of them was smoking a cigarette and the other was letting one of the calves suck his fingers. The feeders were empty and the little things looked up at us expectantly, shuffling against each other.

The two men were wearing brown dungarees with large orange circles front and back. I knew that the former transit camp at Popham was now full of Italian Prisoners of War and that sometimes they were let out to work on the local farms, but this was the first time I had come across any of them. Mr. Ranger would probably have shot them dead.

"Chow, bella," said the Italians, brightening up at the appearance of Julia. I noticed that her cheeks had turned a delicate shade of pink as she stared demurely at the concrete floor.

"Right," I said, in the loud voice that I had heard grown-ups using to foreigners, "let's get these calves fed." The milk mixture was in sacks in the corner of the barn and I went over and started measuring it out and filling the buckets with water. The others still stood in a group, simpering at each other.

"Julia! Lend a hand, remember? I can't do it all by myself."

"Oh, sorry."

The two men followed her with the mournful air of a couple of bloodhounds as she came across to join me. With the sleeves of their prison uniforms rolled up over their hairy brown arms they were soon hefting the buckets to the calf feeders. Once they started they worked quite hard.

"They want to know if we've got any cigarettes," said Julia.

"Well, we haven't," I snapped.

When the calves were nearly fed I looked out of the door and noticed Dominic, the deaf-mute son, sitting on a straw bale in the yard sketching a rooster that was standing on top of the dung-heap. He had a way of smiling sweetly and nodding his head a lot when he saw you, and in sign language he summoned me over to look at his picture. I was standing beside him, admiring the deft brush-strokes with which he had painted the arrogant bird when there was a kind of shriek from inside the barn and Julia came dashing out of the door.

"I want to go home! Come on – quick!"

"Whatever's the matter?"

"I'll tell you later!"

The two Italians stood in the barn doorway showing extravagant signs of dismay as we unhitched the ponies and prepared to ride away. Mr. Ravenscroft, too, was surprised. "Everything all right, girls? Have you been demobbed already?" he asked, leaning on the pitchfork with which he had been bedding down two very clean pigs.

"Would you like some goats milk cheese for your mother, dear?" sang out Mrs. Ravenscroft.

"No thank you, we've suddenly got to go home, I'm afraid."

We dug our heels into the ponies' flanks and cantered off down the grassy track, slowing up only when we reached the spinney. I looked across at Julia who was now extremely pink in the face. "What happened? Did the Italian's attack you?" I asked breathlessly.

"Yes – no – well, one of them tried to kiss me," she sniffed, looking as if she was about to cry.

"Good heavens! What was it like?"

"H – horrible. First he said – he said 'Do you like lerve? And then he grabbed me and sort of – sort of stuck his tongue out."

I shivered and nearly fell off as Robin shied at a squirrel.

"Poor you! Will you tell Aunt Dibby?"

"I don't know."

Julia was still upset that evening and Aunt Dibby, being an intuitive sort of mother, soon got the story out of her. There was a dreadful row and everybody was angry with me for taking her to the farm, as if I had delivered her up as some sort of Vestal Virgin to the Italians. We were forbidden to go there again. It was a wretched end to our innocent little excursion into the Land Army.

When Ruth, the real land girl, heard about it she gave one of her shouts of laughter. "You should see the ones on my farm. Randy little stoats, the lot of 'em. We girls have learned to keep a pitchfork handy when they're around!"

A few days later when everybody had calmed down again Aunt Dibby gave Julia a long, serious, if rather vague, talk about the facts of life. I was glad that such a conversation had never taken place, and was not likely to, between my mother and myself; it would have been dreadfully embarrassing and anyway, as Imogen was to remark many years later, you never do really find out until it's too late.

But I was curious to hear some of the 'facts' second-hand, so that night when we were both in bed Julia gave me a hazy description of our parents' love-making in a kind of stage whisper.

I was astonished. "But don't they die laughing?" I asked.

"No, I don't think so. They seem to take it all quite seriously."

There were to be more men in our lives that summer. As the war dragged on, and British cities were increasingly shattered by German bombing raids, many foreign and Commonwealth servicemen found they had nowhere peaceful to spend their leaves. We were to become a sort of second home to a group of Australian fighter pilots, who were sent to us by the Victoria League in London, but the first to come were some Free French airmen who suddenly arrived for the weekend.

Unlike Mrs. Ravencroft's Italian prisoners they were quite shy and spoke no English, which gave my father an opportunity to practise his French. On the first afternoon, as they sat in the iris garden having tea, he soon turned the conversation to the daring deeds of General Montgomery, one of his heroes.

"Ah, Monty!" he exclaimed loudly, stirring his tea in his usual hectic fashion. "C'est un personage extraordinaire! Parbleu! Il chassera Rommel du desert et ces soldats lui suiveront sans peur!" He sat back in his chair, his blue eyes shining with patriotic fervour; it was not unknown for him to burst into tears of emotion over news of some Allied victory or a speech made by Winston Churchill, another of his heroes.

The Free French sat smiling politely digesting his remarks. They nodded their heads, seeming to agree *en principe* with his statements. My mother re-filled their teacups and stood about awkwardly with a plate of sandwiches. To my embarrassment I could see that she, too, was about to give birth to a French phrase.

"Son beret," she observed, patting her hair. "C'est énorme!"

"Of course it's énorme!" My father would brook no criticism of his hero. "C'est part et parcel de lui!"

The French liked playing tennis, and going for walks across the fields looking at the ponies and cows. Up near Whatnot Wood there was a big cedar, which filled them with glee. They soon shed their uniform jackets and shinned up the trunk.

"Allez, allez," they shouted to each other. Showing the first signs of animation, they walked along the high branches with their arms spread wide, not holding on. I was determined to join them.

"You're mad," Imogen stated. "I shan't catch you if you fall."

The Frenchmen hoisted me up and soon I was following them along the straight branches. Planting my feet carefully and keeping my balance with my arms out straight, I felt like a trapeze artist in the circus. I could see why the foreigners were so exhilarated. It was quite easy when you got the hang of it, but it was an awful long way down.

"Show-off," said Julia cattily when I landed safely back on the ground.

When the Australian pilots started coming on a regular basis to spend their leaves, my mother admitted for the first time that perhaps the house was over-crowded. A caravan was found and lodged in the orchard to take the over-flow. Julia, Susan and I were to be the over-flow. The men stayed in the house.

The caravan rocked when you got into it and smelled slightly of gas, but it was exciting lying in the little bunk beds in the long summer evenings. There was no one to stop us chattering for hours or playing games in the orchard when we had to have a pee behind one of the trees. Fred loved it.

We got fairly good at cooking tinned sausages and eggs on the gas stove and sometimes entertained the pilots there. Physically and mentally exhausted from their long hours in the air fighting the Germans, they would lie on their backs in the long grass of the orchard, in shirtsleeves, smoking and staring up at the blue sky overhead. I imagined they could still hear the drone of advancing bomber formations, and see the sky filled with wheeling and diving fighter planes and the terrible sight of their friends spiralling down to the earth in flames.

In the little galley in the caravan, we busied ourselves with our cooking and dished up amorphous messes on paper plates, which they pretended to enjoy.

We knew that they flew Hurricanes and Typhoons, usually in mortal danger, but they did not want to tell us about their lives back at the airfield. They talked about their families in Australia, the giant blue-gum trees and the hundred mile long breaches. Then they played silly games like hide-and-seek with us round our gnarled old apple trees.

None of the pilots who came to us that summer saw Australia again. Norm and Rex were to last the longest. At twenty-four, Norm was the veteran of the Squadron; he had dark hair and the pale face of a poet and we were all a little in love with him. His pal, Rex, was more of an extrovert, with a round freckled face and red hair.

Rex did like boasting about his exploits in the air, though most of them seemed to happen quite close to the ground. He and his mates dared each other to fly under bridges over the rivers and roads of France, and perform other crazy stunts with planes. He told us how he buzzed German convoys and lone despatch riders on the French roads; vehicles would career out of control as the soldiers leapt off to flatten themselves in the nearest ditch. He would circle and come back to repeat the process perhaps two or three times before letting them have it with a burst of gun-fire. Life was a joke to Rex. One day, going in to the dining room for lunch I saw him twang the strap of Julia's new bust bodice. He was killed when a wing tip caught the side of a bridge on the Seine that he was flying under – a dare too far.

Norm gave us all a thrill one day by flying low over our own house in his Typhoon and waggling his wings. He took an aerial photograph of us all standing on the lawn waving. He was shot down over Holland soon afterwards and posted missing. Much later we heard from his family in Australia that he had died under torture in Nazi Germany. They told us that he and his friends had begun to think of Litchfield as their second home.

Chapter Five

In December 1941, the news from almost every theatre of war was very bad; my parents were among the many suffering personal loss.

My father's nephew, Dick Beckwith, who had given me my most treasured possession, the rating's cap, was killed after his ship, the Prince of Wales, was sunk off Singapore. He and some others managed to get away from the scene of disaster in an open boat, only to be machine-gunned by the Japanese. There were no survivors.

He was just twenty-seven and had recently married a small and charming Wren, Yvonne. The last time I saw him he had been full of laughter and fun, and carried me around on his shoulders, which were all of six feet off the ground. His elder brother was already a Prisoner of War somewhere in Germany; at home in North Devon his mother and sisters were devastated.

At the same time news came that Derek, Karin's dashing fighter pilot husband, had died in a dog-fight over the English Channel. I thought of her and her little daughter seeing him off for the last time in the morning, and being told later in the day that he would never come back. I put on my rating's cap and climbed up into the bare branches of my sycamore tree to have a good cry.

A less personal loss, but one which my father nevertheless felt keenly, occurred in Deptford. One of our ancestors had had a ship built on the Thames with which to repel the Spanish Armada and a local pub had been named after him. Every day Marcus passed the Chichester Arms on the way to his office; although he never went inside he liked to see the ancient building standing there. One night it received a direct hit, and all that was left the following morning was a smoking crater; it was like the death of an old friend.

At home the long Michaelmas term came to an end at last, and we waved Mrs. Carter goodbye for three whole weeks. She was to return to her husband in Sidcup, a place which lay in the path of the German bombers on their way to the London docks. It took a terrible pounding if they missed their target or had a few bombs left over on the way home. One day, as she sat in the bath, the blast from a bomb blew the window in and a shard of glass cut her sponge in half.

Back at Litchfield we children were lucky in that our war games were only make-believe. Julia and I harnessed Robin to the trap and dashed around the countryside on errands – in my imagination facing withering fire as we cantered through enemy lines. Sometimes we played at being bombed in the air-raid shelter; this was the cellar, several feet below ground. In pre-War days it had held some nice bottles of wine. Now it contained a First Aid Kit, some tins of sardines and bully beef, jars of Bovril, packets of cocoa, and a stock of candles and blankets. It was strictly out of bounds, making it all the more exciting. We would sneak down there and put on our gas masks, which muffled the screams of pain as the bombs landed. Julia, a born nurse, dressed our wounds with precious Elastoplast while I bravely handed out provisions as the enemy thundered overhead. Susan was very good at sounding the all clear.

In Basingstoke, in real life, Dr. Houseden's family had a similar refuge. Later on in the war, in the terrible days of the pilotless flying bombs or V2's, Mrs. Houseden drilled her children like shooting dogs. By then people knew that when the doodle-bug's drone cut out there would be seconds to go before it hit the target below.

"On my shout DOWN! Everybody into the cellar," she told the family. She must have developed a sixth sense. One day before anyone else had heard the dreaded drone of the flying bomb approaching she yelled DOWN, and the children scampered as one into the cellar. Minutes later the old Victorian house was flattened, but the family survived intact.

The elder sisters' return for the holidays was very dramatic. It was soon noticed that Cherry was not among the dogs and the children rushing to greet them. She often went hunting in the woods for hours, but she always returned for supper. When night fell there was still no sign of her. Imogen was in a dreadful state. "That beastly farmer's probably shot her for a fox! He's threatened to before, just because she looks like one."

It was a weekend and, on the way back from the station with the fathers, my mother drove down to the farm, but nobody there had seen her.

"People are always disappearing in this house," commented Sue, shivering with cold as we tramped round the garden calling and whistling for the dog. "Look at Jane the other day; she went off for ages."

"That was different; she was only hiding in the stables from all of you," said Imogen spitefully. "Cherry! Cherry! Where are you?" We woke up the bantams who began to crow in the Macrocarpa hedge, thinking it was morning.

"Well, there's nothing more we can do tonight." My father, called off the search and headed indoors to the fire; the unopened trunks were still standing there in the hall. "She'll turn up."

That night in bed with Fred, a warm bundle beside me, I listened to the distant rumble of trains going through the cutting and prayed that she had not strayed down there. I knew the terror she would be feeling.

In the morning she was still missing and Imogen, who had been searching and calling since first light, was red-eyed at breakfast.

"She must have been caught in a trap or a snare. She's probably dead by now!" she sobbed.

We did not know how to comfort her. But for once it was a good thing that we were such an extended family. All day we combed the woods and fields around the house. Uncle Claud had a superior kind of dog-whistle that let out a thin scream. A dog could hear it many miles away. Mr. Brown was the only one of ours that paid any attention to it. And there was still no sign of Cherry.

Lunch was a dismal meal, and in the afternoon I rode down to the Railway Cottages to ask Vince for his advice. He was having his Saturday afternoon nap.

"You try Corpse Wood," he said sleepily, "seen 'er sneakin' down there many a time. That's where she'll be, most like – and you watch out, there's plenty of gins in them there burrows."

I galloped home like Wild Jim McGraw with the posse after him.

Corpse Wood was a dense plantation of fir trees, so named after the tragedy that had happened there some years before. A local young man, crossed in love, had driven his car deep into the wood and gassed himself. It was some time before he was found. By then the body was as stiff as a board with its hands clamped to the steering wheel. The only way to get him and the car out was to drive it, jammed as it was between the trees.

PC Harris was summoned from Overton, a nervous character at the best of times who was reputed to be afraid of the dark. The smell in the car was over-powering. After someone had replaced the battery the poor man had to get into the passenger seat beside the yellow-tinged corpse and somehow start the engine and back the car out of the wood. It took him a long time to get over the experience.

As we drew near to the plantation, in the intervals between calling Cherry's name, I told Julia the story. "It was just such a night as this," I ended with a flourish looking up at the wintry sky.

Julia, burst into tears. "Oh, do shut up."

We were all over-wrought. Imogen had been crying for most of the day. She had already lost one beloved dog this second disaster was too much. It was already twenty-four hours since Cherry had disappeared.

It was quite dark by the time we reached the wood.

"Spread out and make a line," said my father, "and then we'll move in together. Only shine your torches on the ground, we don't want to attract the Germans as well."

The plantation was very spooky. The fir trees stood gaunt and still, unlike the constantly creaking, waving larch stands where we used to go pigeon shooting. We all called loudly and then listened. A rabbit's eye caught up in a torch-beam gave a false alarm.

"Cherry, Cherry, where are you?" wailed Imogen as we moved on again. I hoped we would find her before we got to the place where the young man had killed himself.

Aunt Dibby was some yards off to my left and Julia the same distance to my right. Soon we were in the middle of the wood where there were plenty of dried twigs to trip us up. More than once we stumbled and fell, and the grown-ups torches flickered towards us until we got up again.

We established a routine of calling, stopping to listen, holding our breath anxiously and then sadly walking on. It was after one of these halts that Julia fell over, letting out a cry as she went down. At the same moment, there was no doubt about it, we heard a short sharp yelp. A dog's yelp. "I've found her! I've found her! Here she is!"

"Where? Where? Are you sure?"

"Over here! Yes, it's her! It's Cherry!"

And it was. In the light from our collective torches we saw her. She lay on the ground, feebly wagging her tail, with one of her forelegs held fast in a cruel snare. The fathers quickly released it, but when she tried to get up she couldn't stand. Heaven knows how long she had lain there in terrible pain and she was very weak. Imogen gathered her up in her arms.

"As a matter of fact I can't get up either." Julia had sprained her ankle quite badly when she fell over the dog.

"Oh, you poor darling!" exclaimed her mother. "Don't move. Claud you'll have to carry her home."

Uncle Claud, as a teenager, had been too short to be considered for the Navy. To make himself taller he had climbed ropes and swung from bars in the gym. His height did not increase by very much, but his arms grew very long and strong, like a monkey's. Now he picked Julia up as though she were a featherweight.

"The heroine of the hour," said my father, lighting a cigarette. "Well done! Come on everybody, follow me."

And so we marched away from the dark wood rather like the procession in Peter and the Wolf with Imogen carrying Cherry, the fathers alternately carrying Julia and the rest of us following behind. All we lacked was the music.

The moon came out from behind a cloud as we reached the house, illuminating the scene. My father looked up at the Man in the Moon. "We could have done with you before, old chap."

The trunks of the trees hemmed me in on all sides, trailing their soft branches across my face. I knew I had to get through them to find Julia. She was in there somewhere, sitting in the little black car waiting to die as the poisonous fumes seeped in through the crack in the window. The more I pushed and shoved the more entangled I became ... Dogs lay on the ground watching me with luminous eyes. I put my head down and charged. Suddenly moonlight shone all around me.

"Jane! Jane!" Julia turned on the light and sat up in bed. "Whatever are you doing in the cupboard? Do come back to bed."

"Oh, sorry." I sat down on the floor, draped in fallen clothes, trying to get myself together. "I wanted to stop you from killing yourself in the wood."

"Don't worry, I'm going to live for a very long time and anyway, I'm never going near that beastly wood again."

Fred came over and licked my face. I picked him up and got back into bed.

Cherry was soon able to put her foot to the ground and, unfortunately, to resume her wild ways.

"Bloody nuisance," said my father, "a dog that strays like that."

"Darling!" remonstrated my mother, for Imogen was within earshot.

The trunks with their awful smell of 'school' were unpacked and now the exciting preparations for Christmas could begin. In the kitchen Mrs. Harris pushed the brimming ashtray to one side and made a cake, with the help of Aunt Dibby's stock of preserves. As there was no icing sugar we children made a cardboard cover for it, painted white and decorated with blobs of crimson lake for cherries. Standing on stools we all had a go at stirring the pudding. It turned out to be as leaden as it felt when we tried to push the wooden spoon through the mixture. In the little room off the larder where the water pump lived, amongst the whirling machinery, Imogen was making butter. The big earthenware crock of eggs in isinglass diminished daily.

There were sorties into the woods for holly and mistletoe, and Robin brought home a big fir-tree that was secretly cut down in one of the Hutton-Croft plantations.

Yvonne, cousin Dick's young widow, came to spend Christmas with us. Karin and little Angie came, too. I had quite given up either counting or resenting the number of females in our house. Every bedroom was full. Karin and Angie slept in my father's dressing room. One morning when I went in to see them Angie was standing up in her cot. She had inherited her mother's Greta Garbo voice. "Oh no, I'm vet again," she said, looking down at her nappy.

I changed her and we both got into Karin's bed. She lay back on the pillows: blond and beautiful, but with deep shadows under her eyes. I felt too shy to mention Derek and she did not seem to want to bring the subject up.

"So when did you learn to change a nappy, my darling?" she asked. "I am impressed."

"Oh, I used to practise on Caroline when she was younger. I might easily be a nurse when I grow up, actually."

"Really? So what happened to the Admiral of the Fleet?"

"Well, I'll probably be a sea-going nurse. They need us in the Navy, you know."

"I see." She took hold of a length of my tangled hair and twiddled it round her fingers. "And will they let you in with all this stuff? Shall I trim it for you while I'm here? Then you will be ready for active service."

"If you like. Just a little bit. I don't think it's been cut since last you came."

I suddenly remembered that morning when we had walked down the drive with the pram and talked about the war. I wanted to hug her and burst into tears, but the moment passed as she reached for a packet of cigarettes on the bedside table. "Does your Daddy mind if I smoke in his dressing-room?" she asked, lighting up.

"Of course not, he does anyway, when he's dressing for dinner."

"Dressing for dinner. My darling, you live in a vanished age!"

"Dinner!" cried Angie.

"No, sweetheart, breakfast. Nurse Jane will get you dressed and take you down. And will you bring me a cup of black coffee, my darling?"

By Christmas morning suppressed excitement among us children had reached bursting point. We woke in the dark, feeling the mysterious weight of our stockings at the end of our beds, crackling and rustling. There was prickly holly at the top, some more or less utility presents in between and a lump of coal at the bottom. All of it, sheer magic. Fred was soon submerged in a froth of wrapping paper as we ran in and out of each other's rooms. The parents had made sure that everything was much the same as usual, despite wartime austerity and the presence of the two young war widows in our midst.

Downstairs almost every inch of the house had been decorated and the rooms looked ready for some pagan festival, not the arrival of the Christ Child – hung as they were with great garlands of greenery, red-berried holly, old man's beard, trailing ivy and looping home-made paper chains. In the hall a big bunch of mistletoe dangled from the central beam, and the Christmas tree stood sparkling gloriously with tinsel and baubles in the corner by the piano.

After breakfast Bluebell and the ponies had to be seen to. It was a bright frosty morning. The pig, Robinson IV, had long gone; in fact, one of his legs, dressed in breadcrumbs and stuck with cloves, lay at this moment on the sideboard with several slices missing.

The little Church at Steventon was crammed to the doors.

"Happy Christmas! Happy Christmas!"

Our household filled two pews, and Miranda Armstrong and I could only make faces at each other from a distance. We sang some lusty carols. Rev. Hall, the irascible Parson, seemed subdued by the size of the congregation and the amount of foliage decorating the pulpit. He gave us a short sharp exhortation on keeping our enthusiasm going throughout the rest of the Christian year, but none of us bothered to listen. We were all thinking about the presents under the Christmas tree at home that would be opened after the splendid lunch and the King's broadcast, which crackled at us in his tired, stammering voice out of Mrs. Harris's wireless.

Christmas night at Litchfield was traditionally a time for fooling about, for games and charades, dressing up and dumb crambo – all suffused with the smell of burnt cork for wicked eyebrows and moustaches. This year the elder sisters had decided that some kind of formal but light-hearted entertainment would be more appropriate; something to take the grown-ups minds off the dreadful war.

Rehearsals had begun in the schoolroom a week ago, after days of secret discussions about the programme. As usual, with my loathing for communal activities I had declined to take part, but as time wore on I was becoming jealous of the merry goings-on behind the closed doors of the schoolroom.

"It's great fun, we're doing a play," said Julia in our bedroom. "Why don't you join in?"

"Well, I might. Is there a part for me?"

"Of course there is! We make it up as we go along."

When I sidled in the next morning Imogen greeted me sarcastically:

"Here comes Sara Bernhardt! Everybody scrape and bow."

Ignoring her I settled down to help the cast make tomahawks and headdresses out of sticky tape and hen feathers.

"What are these actually for?" I asked after a while.

"Why, the play, of course."

The play was called 'Home, Home At The Grange or The Difficulties Of Living Together'. The curtain would rise on the Chichester family, or Cowboys, sitting happily in their log cabin unaware of the terror without. At the stage direction 'galloping hooves and general crashing' the door flies open and the Leggatts, or Indians, in blackface and feathers, burst in. A wild skirmish ensues, in the middle of which the door opens again and in waddles a huge brown bear (Gilly). United in fear, the two factions fight off the ferocious animal and afterwards sit down to share a Christmas feast in amicable propinquity.

"Is that all?" I asked.

"No, stupid, that's only the first part."

"I'd rather be a Red Indian."

"You can't, we haven't got enough cowboys as it is."

"What's the second part?"

"I could do a little dance and a conjuring trick," piped up Caroline, bouncing on the sofa. "I do know one."

"You're too young to do a solo," said Gilly. "You can pull up the curtain for the second half."

"That's borwing!"

"It's not, it's very important work."

"There should be music," said Sue, who had quite a talent for Cabaret. "Jane and I could sing that Frances Day song, 'Are you fond of Poker, dear, in the morning no, no, no, no,' or however it goes. They're always playing it on the radiogram."

"Hardly suitable for a Christmas show," said Gilly in a knowing way.

"I think there should be a patriotic theme," said Imogen, biting off a thread.

And so there was. When the repertoire was at last finalised, sitting round the schoolroom table, we all painted the programmes.

"There are no O's in ensemble," said Imogen, looking over my shoulder. Caroline spilt her poster paint.

"If you go on like this you'll have to join the audience," said Gilly, the hardhearted producer.

The performance was to take place in the hall. We had improvised a stage against the bookcases and a flimsy curtain concealed the even flimsier log cabin. On the night the females in the audience sat dutifully and expectantly with their backs to the fire, which for once was not smoking; there were our two mothers, Karin with Angie on her knee, Yvonne, and Mrs. Harris and Beryl and Jessie. The two fathers sat in their armchairs looking as if they would rather be left alone with their newspapers.

Caroline, dressed as a sort of usherette, handed round the programmes. They read.

Christmas Follies by the Litchfield Entertainers:
A play:
Home, Home At The Grange
or
The Pleasures Of Living Together

(This was a tactful change of title)

Interval:

'Roll Out the Barrel':	A. B. Chichester and Private Leggatt
'The Highwayman' by Alfred Noyes:	I. Chichester
'Underneath the Arches':	G. Leake and J. Leggatt
Ensemble:	Patriotic Tableau Vivant

God Save the King

The End

'I'm Hitler! I'm Hitler! Bang bang, you're all dead!'

Imogen's part was the worst. The audience had enjoyed the play and then refreshed themselves in the interval, and by the time she came on they were ready to laugh at anything. 'The Highwayman' had only been thrown in to pad out the programme and was in quite a different mood to the other items. Dressed rather like a ghostly galleon, in an old black satin skirt draped over a lamp shade worn round her waist, she bravely launched into the dreadful tale.

My father was standing up by the fireplace now, picking at his fingers as he always did when he wanted to get in on the action. He was living every moment as his daughter bravely stood her ground against the rising mirth. The Highwayman's thrilling return, galloping down the moon-whitened road to claim poor Bess should have held them all in thrall.

But 'T'lot, t'lot, t'lot, t'lot,' must be the most difficult line in the whole of English poetry to recite with gravity in front of your family. It sent them into shrieks and even my father had to take the silk handkerchief out of the pocket of his velvet smoking jacket and dab his eyes.

Imogen retired mortified to the Green Room/schoolroom as Julia and Gilly took the stage for their Flanagan and Allen classic. I followed her out.

"Never mind," I said, putting my arms round my sobbing sister. "The whole point of the performance is to make them laugh, to cheer them up. You were brilliant."

"You weren't half as funny as they fought you was," said Caroline. "I thought it was quite sad when she shot herself."

"Caroline, I love you," said Imogen, cheering up herself. "Anyway, it made them forget about Pearl Harbour for a while."

The Grand Finale was no laughing matter. The tableau vivant was the sort of thing neighbours like the Colmans at Malshanger and the Portals at Laverstoke used to organise us children into before the war. I only took part because I was allowed to be Lord Nelson.

Applause followed Gilly and Julia out, and we all did a quick change and reassembled on the stage. Gilly stood in the middle as Britannia swathed in a Union Jack and clutching a pitch-fork, Imogen, who had not changed out of her black satin crinoline, was Queen Victoria, Julia my Lady Hamilton and Sue, in her brand new tin hat, a sort of Tommy Atkins.

Caroline pulled the string of the curtain and revealed the ill-assorted group, each of us concentrating hard as we held our patriotic poses.

This time the audience clapped politely, paused, and clapped again. The minutes ticked by. Caroline was supposed to have lowered the makeshift curtain ages ago. My one good arm was aching from holding my telescope to my one good eye and I could feel Britannia's pitchfork wobbling. Julia's face beside me was set in a glassy smile.

Suddenly a small figure with a burnt umber moustache burst out of the wings wielding a toy gun. "I'm, Hitler! I'm Hitler! Bang bang, you're all dead!" cried Caroline. With one accord we broke ranks and chased her off the stage.

"Bravo! Bravo!" The audience dutifully applauded and the dogs came out from under the piano to join us as we made our bows, ruefully pushing naughty Caroline to the front. Shadows of clapping hands fluttered on the ceiling in the firelight and we could see a row of happy faces in front of us. It was over. I was surprised to find how exhilarated I felt at performing in a group of happy faces for the first time in my life.

"We never did sing 'God Save The King'," complained Julia as we changed back into our ordinary clothes.

"I hate 'God Save The King'," said Sue, "It usually makes me cry."

"Then it's just as well we forgot to sing it!"

We went back to the hall where Mrs. Harris and Jessie produced after-the-theatre refreshments, and then retired. We sat by the fire eating biscuits and drinking cocoa and basking in the audience's praise. They had probably been bored blue, but they did not show it.

"Darlings, you were wonderful," said Karin in her husky voice. Baby Angie couldn't stop clapping, and was only hushed when her mother took her off to bed.

We had not noticed that the fathers had left the room, but after a while we became aware of some hoots of laughter and rustling in the passage outside. Suddenly the door opened and a small Scotsman took the stage. He was wearing some sort of kilt that showed his knobbly knees, and black silk socks and sock suspenders, which covered his bulging calves. On his head was a curious kind of bonnet that looked suspiciously like a pair of someone's knickers. He was followed in by a mysterious hermaphrodite figure, draped in a tablecloth, who peeped coyly at us from under a big black hat. She was smoking a cigar and deemed to have rather a blue chin for a lady. We hugged ourselves and waited.

The 'Scotsman' hitched up his kilt and cleared his throat. Behind him the 'lady' had turned her back on us and seemed to be trying to open a door while snorting with fits of giggles.

"There's a Gentleman's Convenience to the south of Waterloo," boomed the Scotsman, giving her a disapproving glare.

"And another one a little further doon.

There's an agitated lady pooting pennies in the slot

While the attendant watches her wi' a froon."

Here there was a lot of business between the two of them before the unfortunate lady, table-cloth slipping, was bundled off the stage, lashing out with her umbrella as she went.

We laughed till our sides ached. The fathers came back with a bottle of champagne and we all had some bubbles in our glasses. I could not remember a better Christmas.

Then, in the general merriment, I saw Aunt Dibby look across at my mother. She had a very short nose, which she wrinkled when she wanted something. She was wearing a paper hat of a particularly vicious pink, which was at odds with her serious expression.

"Myra," she pleaded. "Play the piano for us, do."

My mother went over to the piano and sat down on the stool. She looked up at the towering, sparkling, bauble-hung Christmas tree as if seeking inspiration. We all gathered round. What were we expecting?

Good King Wenceslas? Rule Britannia? She spread her fingers on the keys, waited for absolute silence and then began to play.

'Some day I'll find you,
Moonlight behind you,
True to the dream I am dreaming...'

I looked round the circle of faces leaning over the piano and suddenly another crowd of people seemed to have taken their places – the ghosts of pre-war days. Swaying to the haunting music the couples danced in each others arms, the men wearing dinner jackets, the women in shimmering dresses; there was champagne in their glasses, too, and long cigarette holders in their hands.

Then the vision dissolved and I was back with our homely, shabby wartime Christmas party. The faces of the grown-ups listening to Myra playing were pale and drawn with the strain of the last two terrible years. But tonight they were smiling and their eyes had a kind of shine to them as though they had been bathed in glycerine.

The End

EPILOGUE

By 1944 the tide of war was turning, and it was considered safe for the Leggatts to return to their house in Somerset. Mrs. Carter went back to Mr. Carter in the ruins of Sidcup. She left her pupils with a hazy grounding in geology, archaeology and drawn thread-work; the Turkish Patrol, to whose scratchy tune we had done our horrid P.T., was silent forever.

In my last report Mrs Carter noted that I had approached my schoolwork with a mixture of insecurity and nonchalance. I looked up 'nonchalance' in the dictionary: 'Unmoved, indifferent, cool'. I decided to become even more nonchalant in future.

The house was not empty for long, for the parents had recently joined the Victoria League, an organisation which looked after the welfare of Commonwealth servicemen; we became one of the homes chosen for them to spend their leaves in, far away from their own homes as they were. A contrast to the Leggatts, the Australian and New Zealand pilots who came were quiet, withdrawn young men who slept a lot or sat about in their bedrooms. Some of them became our special friends, and it was heartbreaking as one by one they were killed in action.

On VE Day, Woman Observer Myra Chichester marched through the streets of Winchester in the victory parade and was given a medal by the Air Council. Peace descended on Litchfield Grange, whose walls for so long had been stretched to the limit, but we did not have long to enjoy having the place to ourselves again. In 1946 the landlords foreclosed the twenty-one year lease and in 1947 we left my beloved home, my childhood paradise, forever. The week before we left men arrived in a truck to prise the wrought iron gate, with its intricate leaves and bunches of grapes, off its hinges and take it away. It was the final twist of the dagger.

Now the family was squashed into the two-room flat in London in which the fathers had lived during the war. Fred was our only remaining dog. He refused to go for walks on a lead and one day our mother lost him in Hyde Park. He turned up at Gerald Row police station. We found him, looking very cross, in the arms of the sergeant. He was as disgusted with London life as I was.

Robin and his trap were sent off to live with some cousins in Kent. I never saw him again.

Although my education had hardly begun, - and 'insecure and nonchalant' as I was, I had not surprisingly failed my School Certificate - I was soon sent off to a finishing school in Earl's Court. To ease the strain of our cramped quarters in the flat I boarded there. One night I frightened the headmistress out of her wits by sleepwalking into her bedroom.

I have been *Walking In My Sleep* ever since.

Jane Chichester.